You Are Your Own Beloved

By

Soulfire
Sunflower two

ISBN-13: 978-0-578-33461-5 (paperback)

Dedication

I dedicate this book to you the bravest of brave souls willing to explore knowing that you are God, God is Love and You are your own beloved – I love you. From the bottom-less of my heart, I thank you for supporting and loving me!

Epigraph

"Self-rejection is the greatest enemy of the spiritual life because it contradicts the sacred voice that calls us the 'Beloved.' Being the Beloved expresses the core truth of our existence."
– Henri Nouwen

Flower of Contents

You Are My Reason

I was invited to be a presenter in a sixteen day yoga pilgrimage through the sacred land of Nepal. I brought a group of six yoga students with me. It was an exciting dream come true for me! I had done a pilgrimage through sacred India ten years prior and I expected Nepal to be just as enlightening.

On the first day of the retreat, I was asked to lead a guided meditation in front of about eighty people. I was honored but nervous as I stepped on the stage to start. As I spoke, someone kept switching out the microphone! Apparently it wasn't working? The microphone was replaced three times in the middle of my attempts to guide people into meditation-very distracting to say the least!. To make it worse, no one understood English so mostly everyone was talking instead of following my meditation. I was about half way into the meditation when I brought the palms of my hands together in the center of my heart as a normal part of the meditation and the Nepalese people thought it was over and started clapping.

"Boy what a blunder!" I said to myself as I went to the back of the very large yoga shala to sit on the floor, trying not to feel the embarrassment and humiliation that were starting to creep up.

One of the Nepalese presenters who I had heard give a speech in Nepalese that I didn't understand a word of except for when he would yell, "YOGA," turned to me and said, "You are very connected," looking up. "By the grace of God you are here and you have everything you need to be successful."

My pride was starting to return.

I nodded my head and smiled in agreement at this man I did not know. He continued, "Everything, but love."

Sinking back down, I was not expecting that one! He continued on, "Your family never showed you love."

Shocked at his statement I thought to myself, How on earth did he know that???

"They didn't show you love because they didn't understand you because they never took the time to get to know you. But no matter," he said, "You will always be loved because you were born for the people and they will always love you."

"How do you know that?" I asked him with tears in my eyes. He replied, "I'm a face reader."

And, just like that, my secret pain dissolved and my burden was lifted. He had spoken the words out loud what I've been carrying around in my heart for 49 years.

When he said, **"You are born for the people,"** I felt the words deep in my bones and I knew they were true, that that was my whole reason for my existence. All I've ever wanted to do is heal the world and all sentient beings in it since I was a little girl. His insight made so much sense to me and explained why I never felt connected to my adopted family, never felt loved or understood and carried so much self doubt and insecurity within my being. But that was the "Ah Ha Moment" that gave me something to live for, my purpose...YOU.

I have carried the Nepales' words with me ever since and they have encouraged me to carry on my spiritual journey, even when things were hard, which they often were.

Before I moved to Hawaii I had a little Bon Voyage get together. I had no idea, I really didn't- the cards, letters, notes, hugs, gifts- I received...I have never felt that much love in my entire life. It was so overwhelming, I started to doubt my move! I guess the face reader from Nepal was right, I will always receive love from the people.

I want you to know I took all of your cards, gifts, letters, and memories with me in my heart to Hawaii and when I was feeling lost and uncertain I went back to them. They comforted me when I was feeling alone, gave me strength when I was in doubt, and mostly filled me with love. I cherish every gift, note, card and letter, but mostly I cherish you.

I'm so thankful for you, my dear faithful friends for sharing this crazy earth ride with me. It is both beautiful and heartbreaking, I know! The good news is that when you make a commitment to your spiritual awakening and growth and start to heal, really heal, not on a superficial level but a deeper level, life gets easier and smoother. The struggles dissipate and life becomes a magical ride. This is where I'm at now. The beginning was hard for me, the first 52 years to be exact. Now I'm moving into the state of ease and grace, at last. You too can get there. It is my honor to be your guide.

So come with me as we journey down the corridors of my heart and explore the powerful learning, healing and growth I have had, since you are my reason after all. Yes you.

You Are Your Own Beloved

This is the great Truth that I am committed to helping humanity discover. This is what everyone is consciously or unconsciously searching for, the love within- because the love within is everything.

"You are your own beloved." I sincerely feel this statement represents the most important and sacred work that is needed now on the planet.

You might be wondering, what does "You are your own beloved" mean? Maybe some of you resonate intuitively with this statement, but wonder, how do I become my own Beloved? Maybe some of you already ARE your own beloved and if so, well done!

The word "beloved" consists of two parts: "be" and "love" "be" and "loved." First, we are in a state of being: BE, there is no "do" or "doing." Then there is the word, "love." The word "Love" seems to have as many meanings as there are people who use it. In this book, I use the word "love" interchangeably with the words "divinity," "presence," "God," "All That Is," and "You." Love is a verb, it's not a thing that you own or possess, it is a state of being and who you are in your core essence. Love is the very substance and fabric that every little thing is made out of in the universe- it's the glue that holds the planets in place. Love is the eternal everlasting foundation of life.

Love is the experience of Infinity

Words in themselves don't hold meaning, they are sound vibrations used to describe existence. It's the energy and intention behind them that conveys their true meaning. For example, you could say to your best friend "I hate you," with a smile on your face because you both know the intentions behind the words do not mean what those words state in their conventional meaning. You could also say, "I love you," to someone when you really don't and you feel that through the energy of the words spoken. Some words provoke negative reactions in some people while being revered by others, like "God" and "Love." If a specific word in this book evokes negative emotions, I suggest you replace it with another one similar in meaning that resonates with you.

So, when I say "You are your own beloved," I am also saying "You are God." Twenty years ago, when I first heard "You are God," it made me very uncomfortable. I was brought up Catholic, and was taught that God stood on high outside of ourselves judging all and damning everyone to eternal hell if you cussed (and I cussed a lot!) I grew up listening to Pat Benatar belting out, "Love is a battlefield," so naturally my relationships were filled with mines.

Hypnotized from the day we are born, we are programmed by society, culture, religion, school, our parents, and the media-television. The biggest lie that continues to weave its way into our minds though society and our pop culture is that the search for our true love – our counterpart or our completeness- is outside of ourselves.

It took me time to release the false belief of searching outside myself and replace it with a new one that resonates with me deeply: "I am God." Which can also be stated "[I] You are your own beloved."

As you are reading the leaves of my sunflower, I encourage you to keep an open mind and open heart. Love is not a battlefield, love is a vibratory frequency that is the building block of who you are. God is Love and you are God so you are Love. Love of self is not earned, it is your birthright because love is who you are. And God, well, God is All. But feel free to interchange the word God with Source, Energy, Creator, Goddess, I Am, Best Friend, Divine Intelligence, Lord, Father/Mother, Almighty, Allah, Great Spirit, Consciousness, Universe…whatever floats your boat.

I realize some of the concepts woven throughout might be the first time you are hearing them and you might not understand them. When I read my first metaphysical book twenty five years ago, Seat of the Soul by Gary Zukav, I had no idea what the heck he was talking about-some soul in a seat somewhere? What? But deep down something resonated with me, so I continued. A seed was planted. Years later I went back to it and it made so much sense.

As you read this sunflower note that I share my life stories not in linear chronological time, rather in the way they affected my learning and growth. Think of evolution of consciousness as a spiraling staircase. It is going up but there are times when you have to circle back to re-learn a lesson or go through a struggle again, as you are ascending. The beautiful thing is that as I evolved in my consciousness and healed my trauma I never sunk back down as far and I rebounded much quicker…that's progress.

Reading my story with your heart and not your mind means connecting to the right side of your brain where your intuition lies. This is the opposite of linear left brain thinking. When you read my story in this manner you are absorbing my loving energy and pure intentions coming through my words and the spaces between the words. Your heart is the only true meter that will bring you back to your divinity. Your heart knows what is true.

How do we come to be our own Beloved? First we must ponder the ultimate question, "Who are you?" You cannot be your own Beloved if you have no idea who you are. The journey begins by digging deep to re-discover the inner self that lies within waiting anxiously and eagerly for your reunion....Are you ready?

Welcome to My Heart

Since the publishing of my first sunflower *Fearless Freedom Becoming SoulFire,* I've had a plethora of more "becomings" or deep spiritual real-izations about who I really am which lead to the most significant transfor-mation: "becoming" to "being." The question I asked myself that shifted me into this transformation was, "How many more polarity experiences must I give myself- going down to the bottom, rising to the top, down to the darkness, stripped of all, rising to the light, over and over again until I get it!? I'm exhausted! You get to a point where you say, "Enough!" Why don't I just stay at the top and be the light. You can't spend your whole life becoming something. There's a point in your evolution where you just have to fucking BE it already.

From my first book, you'll know that my logos or imprints are very mean-ingful to me as they are a reflection of my true self and the story of my soul's evolution. In "Becoming" I describe the beautiful twelve chakra sunflower logo. Since then, I received two new sunflowers or logos from Spirit. Each sunflower or logo I've received has represented a rebirth, which are usually challenging experiences that consist of the dark night or many dark nights of the soul. I received two of them since Fearless Freedom was published. That is why I cocooned myself and went off grid these last few years since moving to Hawaii. I was busy being reborn over and over again, ultimately learning how to BE. I have a lot to share that I hope will help you BE, too!

What I learned was that healing and becoming never ends. Life is a continuous process of unfolding. There are many layers, so many deep seeded wounds and traumas that we carry around without even consciously being aware of them. I thought that since I wrote my autobiography and felt this lightness, freedom and peace that I have never felt before, I was free and healed. In a way I was, but there was still more.

I healed my core abandonment issue for sure, as you will see. I am very proud of it by the way, but there was another layer to heal and I didn't even know it! Gratefully, my Hawaiian Beloved and the sacred land of Hawaii/Lemuria showed me.

Lemuria/Hawaii

***Land where the Goddess dwells

HAWAII, WHICH TRANSLATES INTO "LAND where the goddess dwells" is like being on steroids for your spiritual enlightenment. Hawaii (Big Island) represents the root chakra so if you don't deal with your "stuff" the Island will find a way to put it right in your face! Then, you either resolve it and live in harmony with the goddess or not. Manifestation happens quickly in Hawaii; and if you are in alignment with your divine self and doing the inner work, life will be magical. If you're not, it can be a real struggle and is the reason why a lot of people move back to the mainland.

Moving to Hawaii has been the best decision I have made. At first it was a rough go. I moved twelve times within the first two years and questioned my dreams. Now I'm finally in a place where I am rooted and peaceful living in a small but quaint Ohana (In-law/guest house) walking distance to the beach! It's affordable and the best thing it's my own space- no sharing, no roommates, no landlord, just Karma, my dog and the kitty and I. Not only do I feel lighter and happier, I get to thrive in the energy of the goddess Island!

It's almost impossible to be in a bad mood here. Trust me, I've tried. There have been rough times like I said, but no matter how hard I tried to be upset and angry I just couldn't stay in that vibration. If you pay attention you will see everything around you is emanating love, light, joy and beauty. I'm very connected to the land (Aina in Hawaiian), to Pele the Goddess of the Fire, the ocean, the mountains, Mauna Kea, the banyan trees, dolphins, whales, sea turtles, owls, flowers, all of nature. It is a magical and sacred place to live and the perfect climate for nature lovers like me. The Aina has supported me in my healing, and I will forever be grateful.

***My True Love

My move to Hawaii fulfilled several deep desires I've had all my life. I decided long ago that in this lifetime I would only live on islands. I grew up on Long Island, moved to the Big Island, and went to college in Rhode Island. I know it's not technically an island, but it's close enough! On the Big Island is where I completed my search for the Beloved and became a "self contained island," finding my security, happiness and love within.

The ocean is my refuge, just the smell of it brings me home. I would go to the ocean in the winter, spring, summer and fall. It didn't matter how cold it was. I shared my life with the ocean, every part of it, the good, the bad, the heartache, and the sad. I poured my heart into the ocean, my tears, my laughter, my joy, and my appreciation. Whenever I am by the ocean I feel at peace. No matter what crazy is happening in my life, when I am beside the ocean everything is okay. I am most in touch with my heart and my pure state of resonance in the ocean.

"You will always be my first true love," I would say to the ocean. Usually I followed it up with the thought, the man that ends up by my side will have to understand this.

Don't get me wrong, I love the mountains and the trees too. I find peace there as well, as I do in all nature, but the ocean is the embryonic fluid of Gaia, it is from where we are born to where we are returning, to the mother's womb.

We are returning to the mother of us all, to the ancient sacred land where we once lived in harmony with the divine feminine energy, in harmony and honor with one another and all living things, in oneness and unity. Hawaii is Lemuria, the sacred ancient lands that sank underwater thousands of years ago. It's the land where the first humans lived. Since all I have ever wanted to do was evolve in my consciousness it makes sense that I felt drawn to Hawaii/Lemuria.

I have traveled all over the world, but Hawaii was the first place I visited where I felt like I belonged. I didn't stand out and the people here didn't make fun of me, like they did on Long Island. I was treated the opposite way, they thought I was a local and that brought more respect. It was such a different experience than growing up with an adopted family that all had blond hair, blue eyes and white skin. My soul felt safe in Hawaii so after my first visit twenty years ago I swore one day I would be back to live.

***The Big Island

There are eight different Hawaiian Islands so when I first moved, I wasn't sure which one I would end up on. My daughter had relocated to the Big Island so I went to visit her for Christmas the year my memoir was published in 2017. I told my daughter at that time that I would probably move to Maui, not the Big Island. She was positive I would want to be on the Big Island and she was proven right! From the moment I arrived on the Big Island it spoke to me. I received divine guidance and intervention that saved my life.

After a very long trip from New York I arrived around 10pm and rented a car to make the hour and half drive to my daughter's place in Oceanview. I had not anticipated that I would be exhausted from the trip and would have to drive unknown roads at night when I am not a good night driver. I was just so excited to finally be back in Hawaii. I was driving down the dark highway with the windows rolled down and a huge smile on my face.

I was completely shocked when a car driving on the other side of the highway suddenly turned and came over the double yellow line right toward me! The car's headlights were blaring in my face and it was going about 50 miles per hour. I screamed, swerved to the right to avoid the collision then came back on to the highway. Shaking in my whole body, I was baffled as to why this had happened. I am finally here after all these years, back in Lemuria and this is my greeting? Was this an omen? Does the island not want me here? I questioned. My mind went on a wild goose chase.

A few minutes later I would understand why.

The road changed quickly from a straight wide highway to a one lane windy dark road with no street lamps and a speed limit of 25 MPH. My heart jumped out of my shirt when I looked to the right for a glance at the ocean and realized it was a cliff. (OMG!) I am also afraid of heights so this freaked me out even more. I was getting sleepy and had to keep pulling over to get out of the car to walk around and breathe. It was brutal. Finally I called my daughter to tell her I might not make it, that I would just sleep in the car so I don't drive over a cliff.

I ended up continuing my journey and making it to my daughter's place. It took me twice as long but I was alive in one piece! I realized the urgency and dramatic sign I received from that car was a warning-guidance that potentially saved my life. The rest of my visit to the Big Island was the same- synchronicities, divine signs, guidance, connection and magic everywhere! I knew that my daughter had been right and that this was the island I was going to move to. Archangel Michael even had his own church here! Since he is my guardian angel I thought there couldn't be a better sign.

My secret deep desire to move to Hawaii was at last fulfilled... Now I had just to fulfill my last secret desire: to find my true love...which I did.

***Guy Island

Guy Island is another name for the Big Island. I was told that for every girl there are three guys. I believed it because they seemed to be coming out of the woodwork when I first moved here, but they all seemed off in some way. Spirit shared with me that I was meeting fragments because I still had not become the beloved of my own heart.

It seemed I still carried some baggage with me after the advice I received from my wise friend in Long Island before I moved. At my going away party she made it a point to pull me aside and share a message from Spirit. She told me that I could not step foot on the sacred land of Lemuria carrying any baggage- that I was not to bring "my stuff" with me to this pure holy land. I took her advice and did some sessions with healers and made sure I was in the right space, but apparently not enough.

Before I met my Hawaiian Beloved I had some initiations to go through. The Big Island is the youngest of all the Hawaiian islands. It is the home to four active volcanoes so the land is always changing and growing because of the lava flow. Lava is a stone of rebirth and transformation. It makes sense why I landed here.

The people of Hawaii believe that everyone goes through an initiation or test from Pele, Goddess of the Fire, when they first move to the Islands. Pele, also known as Madame Pele, shapes the sacred land through destroying and creating land. Pele's tests are no joke. Pele exposes the shadows inside and will chew you up and spit you out if the shadow is not dealt with. Pele's tests send many running to the mainland.

***The Holy Land

I had my share of Pele's initiations. I started my happy journey to paradise in, what my daughter called, a "rustic" cabin, which was really another term for upscale glamping. I welcomed the rustic cabin and all the mosquitos with open arms the first day and night. I even said to my landlord, "I don't mind that the mosquitos bite me, I am a host for their nourishment." Yea, I said that. That lasted two days.

By day three I was done. "I can't take the mosquitos, the ants crawling everywhere, the bugs in my bed. The mosquito net doesn't do shit and my shower has only one temperature, scalding hot!" I whined. The initial "glow" of Paradise was slowly wearing off.

My gracious landlord, who really wanted me to stay, offered to have me spend a trial night in the tree house – the other rental on the property. My daughter had spent a few nights in the tree house already and warned me that she wasn't able to sleep because of the loud trucks driving by during the night on the highway, and the rats crawling across the transparent roof.

No matter, I thought. I can handle it. Anything that had closed in walls with windows and doors was a step up for me at this point. So I moved. While it took an entire day to clean the rustic cabin, cleaning the tree house took me an entire week. Cleanliness had a different definition in Hawaii I was starting to learn. (It reminded me of India, but not as extreme.) I threw my back out cleaning, which I hadn't done in years, but I kept going. The tree house had a wrap around lanai (porch), a walk-in closet and Direct TV! I was living large and how cool was I, living in a treehouse! I was content.

The glamour of living in a tree house soon wore off as soon as I was face to face with a mouse on my yoga mat, cooking in a kitchen crawling with ants, and stuck watching rats with long ass tails crawl over the roof at night. My sound machine had no chance against the monster 18 wheel trucks that shook the entire tree house during all hours of the night. My daughter's warning was right. Plus there was the torrential rainfall that was so loud I couldn't hear the TV while sitting directly in front of it with the volume at the highest level.

The adjustment to my brand new life in the middle of nowhere was challenging coming from New York. I was in such a secluded part of the island and the only store was a general store from the 1900's where you bought everything: food, produce, gas for your car, tampons, beer. Town was basically the ACE hardware store. Karma my dog had an emergency vet visit and I had to drive an hour and half just to get there. Don't get me wrong, it was a beautiful and special part of the island, I was just not used to living in such remoteness. Did I mention there was nowhere near where I could get into the ocean safely.

I called my brother Sita (Sita is my brother/sister/spiritual guide who I will be referring to throughout) lamenting over my situation and the only thing she asked me was where do I get my hair done? My hair!? Really?! That was the last thing I was concerned about! She thought I was a little coo coo for moving to such an isolated area.

One night over the ear piercing rainfall, I heard a gunshot. I was so scared, I called my landlord to tell him the neighbors just shot a gun and he replied, "Oh that was an avocado falling on your roof." The next day my landlord sadly informed me his dog had drowned in the pond in our front yard. I hurriedly packed a suitcase, borrowed his minivan and drove to the AirBnb I had rented in Kona. I was in tears. This is not how I imagined the start of my dream life in Hawaii.

Even though I had this fantasy in my mind of living alone in the middle of nowhere writing my book, it turns out I like people after all. I realized as much as I enjoy my alone time I needed balance. I needed to be social and be around people too. I also needed the sun, town, shops, and signs of life! The Kona side of the Big Island had everything I wanted and it was where I decided to settle down. It's a quaint little town with everything you need. I could take Karma out at 8pm for a stroll through town and feel safe. And the best part is I can get in the ocean, swim, snorkel. paddle board, boogie board, and surf every day to my heart's delight.

Nonetheless, the initiations were not over...

***Adult College

I rented a room in a large house with four other housemates that was also an AirBNB rental. At times there could be six to eight people in the house. It was busy. At first I loved it! It was fun to have company around, I never felt lonely, and I always had someone to do something with or eat a meal with. It was really nice at first. We all got along, until we didn't.

And that's usually how the story goes. It went south pretty fast. The Brazilian housekeeper who lived in the camper in the back was very jealous of me, and it didn't help that she was an alcoholic. Her fake kindness turned into outright rudeness. She would walk by me and say,

"Get a real job," when I was writing on the porch just minding my own business.

I pretty much ignored her and didn't let her bother me. I knew deep down she was a mess, so I didn't take it personally. But then she started messing with my dog Karma and I had to draw the line. We got into it, and it was a lot of drama. The next time she saw me and said to me, "Get a real job."

I responded, "Why don't you get a job?" Since I did all the cleaning in the house she was supposed to be doing.

She replied, "I have two jobs."

Oh yea, what are those? I thought to myself. *Blow job and hand job?* Cuz she definitely was not working as our house keeper for her rent. I know it was a mean thing to think but the drama was unbearable at this point. I eventually had to move.

***With conflict comes silver linings if you look for them

I was staying temporarily at a friend's house and living out of my RAV4 while trying to find a new home. One evening I was at the local Magic Sands Beach watching the sunset with Karma and I fell asleep face down in the sand. I guess all the drama exhausted me more than I knew. Karma was on leash but got up and started barking at some people walking by.

I was woken up, startled, by a man yelling angrily at me, "No dogs on the beach!"

The anger seemed so out of place in such a serene moment of the sunset. I had also seen plenty of people bringing their dogs to the beach after the lifeguards had left, so I was kind of annoyed by the man. No longer able to enjoy the beach I went back to my car to leave. I noticed the man who yelled at me standing by his truck. He was a local large dark skinned man.

A moment of clarity shined through, remembering the message from my sister friend before I moved here about bringing your baggage to the holy land. I said to myself, This island, this land is sacred. You moved here to bring peace and light. You cannot leave this situation unattended with negative conflicting energy hanging around. You must be the light, be the change. Fix this.

Acting on my intuition, I took a deep breath, got out of my car, bravely walked over to him and sincerely apologized. I said, "I'm sorry if my dog disturbed your zen. It's just that we are in between homes right now and I fell asleep. My dog is usually quiet and well behaved."

His angry face immediately changed. He responded with such kindness, "Yes ma'am," he said, "Is there anything I can do to help you?"

I wanted to cry. My shoulders dropped and I relaxed. I introduced myself and we became fast friends. I had no idea how much this angel was indeed going to help me.

The next day I pulled up to the beach and he was there again. He walked over to say hello and asked me if I was ok, noticing the strained look on my face.

I told him, "NO," with tears in my eyes.

I explained to my new friend that my belongings were in the house I had just moved out of. My things were locked in my friend's room who was away on vacation, however the manipulative landlord texted me to tell me he moved my things to a storage facility and once I paid him for it he would give me the key – which was an outright lie. I was beyond angry. I couldn't believe this was happening. He was a sixty five year old grown man.

My new Angel friend came to my rescue. He told me to call the police and that he would go with me to help me get my things back. It was a sight to see, a convoy of four SUVs pulling up to my old landlord's house, with two police, my Angel friend and myself. My Angel friend stayed with me and calmed me down as the police interrogated the landlord who lied and said I never lived there. Luckily for me, the sneaky landlord's reputation preceded him and along with the chain of text messages he had sent me proved he was a liar. The police told him to back off and let me get my things or he would be arrested.

My Angel friend stood by and loaded his truck with all my suitcases and belongings, which was a lot more than I thought! He drove my things to his house and stored them in his garage. He showed me how to access the garage and let me know I could keep my stuff there for as long as I needed.

I was overwhelmed with gratitude. I hadn't even been in Hawaii for three months and couldn't believe how much drama I was experiencing. He and the police went out of their way to help me. The police didn't have to help me as this was a civil issue they told me, but they did anyway. I knew I was being watched over and protected.

I turned a potentially negative situation into one of healing for both my Angel friend and I. I gave my new friend an opportunity to do a kind act, and to show aloha to a stranger. In his giving he also received. It was a win-win all around.

And Brazil? Well she stood there at the door as I was grabbing my things and running out of the house talking badly about me to the police and chanting "Ew," each time I walked by.

"EW YOU!" I fired back in front of the police. I didn't care. I was so tired of her rudeness. It was a complete 'shit show.'

Funny thing is that a year later Brazil and I ended up working at the same spa together. She came up to me and apologized for her behavior. I thought that was really awesome. We hugged it out. I had no bitterness or resentment toward her. I knew she was struggling deep inside and I was practicing not taking anything personally.

One of the things I learned about living on a small island with a small population is to not burn bridges. Keep everything "aloha" and the island will take good care of you.

A GATEWAY TO BEING YOUR OWN BELOVED – BYOB

***Honu Heart

The initiations kept going and the island continued to guide me. The Honu, Hawaiian for Sea Turtle, came to me. She is one of my Amakuas. Amkua in Hawaiian is a spirit guide. I was sitting on the beach at the water's edge one evening still in search of a place to live when all of a sudden a sea turtle came up to my feet. Startled, I jumped back. She came up to me again. I moved back again. She kept coming out of the water and right up to me. I stayed still and let her find her space on the beach. She parked herself right next to me. I sat there in silence and gratitude with her, just taking in her energy, the beauty and the sacredness of the moment. *What is it that you've come to tell me, Honu?* I asked her silently.

Home is in your heart holy child. When you find home in your heart, your physical home will appear like magic. ~Honu

***The Sacred Refuge Within

There are different variations of retreat centers all over the world. You might have gone to a retreat center where you've walked into the building and felt the energy of serenity and peace and maybe participated in a retreat there that made you feel exhilarated, connected and alive, but when you got home those feelings slowly dissolved and you were back into the same ole same ole. This happened to me quite frequently in my quest for inner peace.

I realized some years later why this phenomenon was happening. It was because the hard drive was not upgraded...meaning somewhere in my subconscious mind I had not made the change. I was still holding erroneous beliefs of lack and unworthiness. That is why we must do the inner work. No matter where you go, you take your consciousness with you. There's no escaping it!!

The most important retreat center one can attend is the one within the center of one's being. "Home is in your heart," means finding the retreat or refuge within your inner being, your sacred heart womb. When you have that, no matter what's happening in the outer world, you will remain happy, empowered and free. In your heart you are whole. In your heart you are home. In your heart you are free. In your heart you are complete.

Like the Honu who carries her home with her wherever she goes, our refugee must be within, then our true home is always with us. When you have this type of security you will never be homeless. You might be houseless, but never homeless. I had to change my choice of words.

I understood this timeless and valuable wisdom, however understanding it and applying it are two different things. I spent the next few days in meditation with the intention of going within to find my peace and inner security, and my home. I had been working on this one for a while so it wasn't surprising that a physical home came to me a few days later. Honestly, I think spirit just felt bad for me and was giving me a break. I needed a place to rest my head and it was Christmas Eve already.

***Goddess White Tara

When I first went to check out the new place, the price was a little high, but it was brand new and it was the first place I didn't have to clean. That was a huge factor but the icing on the cake was the ocean view from my bed and the framed picture of the Buddhist Divine White Tara hanging on the bedroom wall. I'll take it!

White Tara is often referred to as the Mother of all Buddhas. She represents the motherly aspect of compassion. Her white colour indicates purity, but also indicates that she is Absolute Truth, complete and undifferentiated.

> When we're open and quiet, universal guidance and timeless
> wisdom is transmitted to us in a thousand ways from a
> thousand beings.

***My First Spiritual Awakening

I had originally moved to Hawaii with the intention of finishing my second sunflower. However, my spirit guides told me my second book was in a holding pattern because I was in a holding pattern. They planted the seed of becoming the beloved of my own heart first, and reminded me that I had to actually "BE it" before I could write about it or it won't be authentic. Ok, Ok. Why do they always have to be right! I thought to myself despite knowing in my heart the truth all along.

Excited to have a beautiful, clean, peaceful Ohana with a view of the divine ocean, I got to work immediately. Time to root and rise. This was my first home in Hawaii where I had my spiritual awakenings.

It was my mission to evolve in my consciousness, so I sat and meditated everyday, but things seem to be awry. I experienced a lot of frustration. While I had this beautiful new space, I also had a lack of money abundance and felt alone and deflated. I was back in my illusionary mind and mind loops. Without consciously being aware of it I had been holding on to this mental fantasy that Hawaii, the land and the people were going to be the deliverer of my abundance and my savior.

It wasn't until I was sitting in my new space, in the lack of it, alone and deflated, that I realized two things. One, this paradise was not going to save me- no island, no land, no people, no man was going to save me;

and two, I was the one giving myself this experience of complete lack. I (my higher self) was giving myself the experience of nothingness so I could sit with it and be with my own consciousness to unfold and fully peel away the layers to the core essence of my being in order to find the security within my own heart.

Genius! This was a whole new level in consciousness. This was self mastery at its finest-when you are in it-and know in the back of your higher mind that this is YOU creating this struggle for yourself so you can recreate something different.

I got up to dance.

I was singing and dancing to the song, From Now On, by Hugh Jackman, from The Greatest Showman and feeling happy that I was finally home in Hawaii, when it hit me. It wasn't about Hawaii being my home, it was finding my true home within me. I was returning to the home in my heart.

> "Your visions will become clear only when you can look into
> your own heart. Who looks outside, dreams; who looks
> inside, awakes." ~CG Jung

The honu's message had finally sunk in. In that moment all the teachings, all the wisdom, all the times I heard "All you need is within," went from my intellect to my heart and into my body. I got it.

I cried and cried. Seems like a theme in my life, but this time they were tears of joy. Home at last. It was a day to celebrate. I felt liberated and secure like I had never felt before. It was a very satisfying and joyful moment. I kept dancing, so happy and feeling free.

Indeed I gleaned my sovereignty in the solitude of the sacred land of Hawaii, but to make this epiphany stick I called in the catalytic counterpart.

The Hawaiian Beloved

"There is an echo from within that says, Yes, I remember
you. Yes, I know who you are, and I know we have been
together before. I don't know where, but I feel and recognize
your vibrations and your energy signature. You touch my
Soul and make my heart strings sing. Your loving Essence
assures me that I am no longer alone. Welcome into my heart.
I ask you to share my journey and to allow me to be a
part of your journey as well."

***The Health Food Store

WE MET OUTSIDE A HEALTH food store. It was exactly five days after my spirit guides gave me that oh so good advice (which I ignored): Once I become my own Beloved I will meet my perfect energetic match since I was still struggling with the unbalanced men that kept showing up. I thought, That was fast! I must be doing a lot of healing and transforming here and ready for my perfect energetic match. I was fooling myself, of course, but had no idea at the time.

I'll never forget that day. I woke up that morning not looking forward to a day of driving eight hours to pick my daughter up on the other side of the island. A mother's duty calls, I reminded myself, and an adventure around the island. And it certainly was.

On the way to drop my daughter off at her home she asked me to stop at the health food store. I waited for her outside, standing with a dog leash in each hand. My dog, Karma on one side and Lotus, my daughter's dog, on the other. Arms outstretched, people watching, waiting patiently for my daughter when I noticed him noticing me from about forty feet away. He was staring at me. As he got closer he looked into my eyes, then away, and then he did a double take and looked right back into my eyes, then entered the store.

That was weird, I thought. He came back out of the store before my daughter, and I don't think he even had any food in his hands.

Approaching me he asked, "Do I know you?"

I replied. "No." thinking, here we go again.

We started chatting easily like two long lost friends catching up after years. He showed me his native feather tattoos on his arms as he noticed the native feathers in my hair. I casually mentioned that it was my birthday next week and I was planning to do a spiritual trek to Pololu- also known as "Valley of the Gods." He said he would like to join me on the trek and that he would be in Kona (my side of the island next week). I thought he was very forward and had wanted to do the hike alone. I decided to stay open because the conversation was both unexpected and refreshing. As my daughter emerged from the store, I gave him my card and said goodbye.

Tainted from the unbalanced men I had already met, I didn't have high expectations, but something about him seemed different. When we talked he seemed so present, he looked directly into my eyes and listened, really listened. He felt solid and much more engaged than all the other guys I had met.

He texted me later that day to say it was nice to meet me. I waited until the next day to call him. We ended up talking for two hours! Then every day after that we talked until his cell phone battery died out. A person's voice tells a lot about their energy and persona. His voice was strong and comforting. It was a good sign.

He worked on his farm land that was off grid on the other side of the island where I was living. I had just settled into my new apartment on the west side of the Big Island in Kona. After eight nights of talking until his cell phone died, he arrived at my doorstep. I felt like I knew him so well already. We spent my birthday at the Valley of the Gods. There was a strong connection. He felt so familiar and easy to be around, yet at the same time, something did not feel entirely right. I wasn't sure what that was.

> "Everything that irritates us about others can lead us to an understanding of ourselves." ~ CG Jung

*** Behold God

After we spent a week together I pushed him away. I told him, straight out, New York style I just wanted to be friends and that he irritated me.

He told me he loved me and he was in love with me. I thought, That was fast.

I repeated straight to his face that I thought he was irritating and just wanted to be friends. He persisted by asking if we could at least be lovers. Ew no.

My wise daughter and Sita both reminded me that we are irritated by others because of something that is within us. The irritation is not from the other person but from within ourselves. Deep down I knew they were correct so I decided to meditate on this insight and truth. I can't get away with anything!

After sitting with my irritation of him, I had a profound vision and experience. I was doing my usual morning reading and meditation, this particular reading was from Jesus. I put my book down and sat in the energy of Jesus's words. I closed my eyes, took a deep breath and immediately felt this surge of energy come into my heart. My body started shaking and hot tears began streaming down my face. I repeated what I had been reading in Jesus's teaching, "Behold God," and another surge of energy went through my entire body.

One by one the face of every person who had "wronged me" since I had moved to Hawaii began to appear in my mind. As I looked into each of their eyes I said, "Behold God," and the face went away and another one came across the screen of my mind. This continued until any person I had negative feelings towards had been seen in the light of God, (and there were quite a few!)

Then I said, "Behold God," for myself and just started crying like a baby, sobbing deep relief from my soul. I am an expert in tears and crying so I knew this one was significant.

The experience left me with such a profound sense of peace that I had never felt before. I prayed that the peace would last. That day I went around saying silently to each person I saw, "Behold God." It was quite a powerful practice that left me feeling high like I was floating through the ethers.

After that profound transformation, I spent the day with my daughter. Usually we would get into little arguments when we spent time together, but not that day. I felt so content and peaceful. I didn't share the experience with her because I have learned that once you start putting words to a spiritual multi-dimensional experience it takes away from the potency of it. I decided to keep it for myself for now and just enjoy being in the peaceful energy with her.

It continued to be a beautiful day. We swam in the ocean together which is not something my daughter likes to do, but she did it for me. I showed her how my HB (Hawaiian Beloved) taught me to boogie board. She laughed at me, a grown woman on a boogie board crashing into the feets of all the adults standing at the water's edge. Oddly, I could not stop talking about my HB with my daughter.

I realized my daughter and brother were right after all! The irritation I felt towards my Beloved was from within myself. I also realized that even though our energies were different, that was okay. I was very calm and peaceful inside and he had more fragmented ADD energy, but I decided there was something else there for me to explore. Feeling a tug at my heart, I called him and asked if I could see him again.

***The Soulmate – A Misunderstood Connection

That second chance started our two year two month journey together, during which time, I came to know that he and I are soulmates. We are part of the same soul family and have been together in many, many, many incarnations. Soulmates are not the romantic Hollywood fairy tale we are programmed to believe. Soulmates can be quite the opposite. They can come with a lot of triggers and therefore, a lot of work. We incarnate in soul groups or families, so we have many soulmates, not just one.

Soulmates aren't always forever either, like we are programmed to believe. Soulmates can come into our lives for a fleeting moment to help us learn a quick lesson. Sometimes they stay for a long period of time to be a huge catalyst in our growth. They provide the triggers to let us see where we need to heal, and then when there is no more growing to do with that being, the relationship changes. But, even if the soulmate relationship changes in the incarnation, the connection to the Soul Family never does. The form/container might change, i.e., you might go from lovers to friends, but does that mean the love changes or goes away? No.

Love never dies

***Back in the Fire

We had a bumpy ride together from the beginning, which is common with soulmates. I was back on the emotional roller coaster. However, I didn't lose myself entirely, like I have in past soulmate relationships. I told him right from the start that I wasn't your typical girl and this wouldn't be your typical relationship. I told him, "I know who I am and what my divine purpose is and I intend to follow it until the day I die. My purpose is the most important thing to me, over a man or relationship. If we could be in harmony together and flow together, great, but it was going to be anything but 'normal." I didn't scare him off with that declaration. That was a good sign.

Still, deep embedded patterns are hard to break. As I began to get comfortable with him I drifted down the road towards losing myself...again. He told me he would take care of me, pay my rent and support me while I pursued my divine purpose. How nice would that be! Being a sole breadwinner and provider as a single mother, his declaration was a welcome change. This is what I had asked for and the universe delivered. So I said, ok.

I was falling into the same pattern again without even knowing it- mentally projecting him as my knight in shining armor who was going to sweep me off my feet and save me. And in a way he did.

In the beginning he was wonderful to me. I keep thinking, Wow, is this man for real? He embodies the masculine and feminine energies. He is so sensitive and sweet and kind and just wants to nurture and take care of me, yet he is fiercely strong and protective of me. I felt safe with him. Me, not so much – I was pretty tough on him from the start. He cried a lot in the beginning and said it was because he was in love with me and couldn't help it. I was irritated by his crying. He told me I needed to be less New York and I told him he needed to be less sensitive. We were quite the couple. It seemed our roles were reversed.

He liked to give me "constructive criticism" as he called it. I did not receive that well at all. I told him the word criticism comes with a negative energy and I didn't like it. We argued about this and a lot of other things. We were both 'alphas' which led to power struggles often. As much as there was an instant attraction and connection, there was also some disconnection in our communication and how we related to each other.

I gave him a hard time about a lot of the things he did, my own form of criticism. I drove him crazy, pushed him away and broke up with him many times over the two year two month journey together. He told me I crushed his soul, but no matter what, he came back, even after he met Tsunami Soulfire. (I was still working on controlling the storm apparently.) That's gotta say something. Was I testing him? Or was I sensing something else? He loved me and I knew it. I felt his presence and his solidity. He was my rock, literally.

***The Sea Maiden

The summer before I moved to Hawaii I had a spiritual session on the beach on Fire Island with Sita. Sita is a high dimensional being and pure channel who's my sister/brother/spiritual guide. We're part of the same soul family and we have been together in many lifetimes usually as brothers and seekers of the light. My guides told me she/he's the only one I listen to, hence the reason she/he incarnates with me. During that session one of my many incarnations was revealed to me: the Sea Maiden. I came to know why the sea was so meaningful to me, and why I had such a profound and deep connection with it.

"You were the wise one," Spirit said, "The wise sea maiden found perched on a rock bathing in the sun. When the ships would come in and gather around, you would bring yourself up to the surface of this rock to radiate the wisdom of your hearts knowing to the seamen to give a blessing. You would deliver divine love energy out to gather in their hearts to bring to the mainland. They would look at this as a great gift delivered from the Gods above." Wait for it, this might be hard to swallow, but I came to learn that my Beloved was that rock. I mean Wow. He was the literal rock I perched upon!

My Capricorn earth Beloved helped me, the emotional Pisces water, overcome so many insecurities, wounds and fears in our relationship. He was my rock and security. I felt safe and loved by him which allowed me to speak up for myself and set healthy boundaries without being scared he would leave me. And as much as I pushed him away, he never abandoned me. If it wasn't for his enduring love and devotion I would never have healed this last major deep seeded wound: part of me was still looking for love and wholeness externally.

PETAL 3

Archetypes

***Human

I LEARNED THE MAIN ARCHETYPE I came into this lifetime was to be the heart centered rooted human. For someone who likes to dream and live in their imaginary mind with the unicorns, dragons, fairies and wizards in the 4D (dimension) plane this was kind of a Debbie Downer at first. I thought maybe my legs were going to morph back into a fin and I would return to the sea as the sea maiden once again here in Lemuria, but no, that was not happening.

I came here to feel the rawness of being human, to be the rooted human in unity consciousness and pave the way for others to be the same. What does being a heart centered rooted human in unity consciousness mean exactly? Living in the rawness of being human whilst knowing you are God; Being rooted in the security of your own heart; Not depending on outside validation or confirmation for what you are feeling inside; Having a divine balance of masculine and feminine energies and balance of the mind and the heart; Thinking with clarity through the portal of the heart center, not the ego mind; Being in true resonance with your Christos heart.

After I finally accepted this truth I decided to fully embrace my humanness. After all it's not easy being human especially when you have forgotten who you are and live in a world that also has forgotten or tries to keep the truth from you. I knew this would be a challenging task while the majority of humans were asleep and unaware of the divine within them. Even my acquaintances and friends who are on a spiritual path were still not fully awake.

I felt I had a big task before me, but this is what I chose- to be a teacher of the divine light- to help souls awaken to the divine within. While this resonates with me fully I'm also aware of the challenges of this mission... starting with me.

***The Unstable Mind, Great...

I love my human mind. It is smart, sharp, focused, organized. It gets things done. And I'm grateful for it.

But sometimes it works against me.

I learned one of the things I came into this incarnation with was an unstable mind. I've been told by my spirit guides that I have been incarnating on Gaia since the beginning and I am very connected to the collective (humanity). The collective mainly lives from the ego mind and not from the heart. So being the warrior master I am, it was my choice to come into this lifetime to slay the dragon, so to say, or to get the unstable mind under control to create new energetic pathways for others to follow. It's no easy feat. It's taken me almost twenty years to get my mind under control, and I'm still working on it everyday.

One thing became clear though, I've spent so much time in my spiritual journey focusing on my mind and thoughts which is the primary focus of yoga and Buddhism, I realized there's a major component missing from these teachings. What about your heart?

***Heartfulness

The whole world talks about "mindfulness." It's all the rage, the new fad, on the cover of Time, celebrities tout it, mainstream media is all over it. I believe this is another way to keep us disconnected from our true strength: our heart. Why don't we call it heartfulness instead of mindfulness?

One day during meditation I had an epiphany. I started chanting, "I believe in myself, I believe in myself, I believe in myself." over and over again. Then I asked myself, "What about you do you believe in, do you believe in your mind or your heart?" I put my hands over my heart center and knew the answer.

I burst out in tears. "I believe in my heart," I said with 100% conviction. I know my heart, I know how pure and good and full of love and caring and compassion it is. I also know any time I need strength or energy it comes from my heart, not my mind. It is because of the strength in my heart, I was able to get through the trauma and darkness in my past and still be a light for others.

Suggestion for meditation: Place your hands over your heart center and take slow deep breaths in and out of your heart. If you are having trouble quieting your mind, inhale into your heart center and exhale through your crown. Visualize the thought forms leaving through the top of your head as gray smoke as you exhale. You can visualize inhaling white light into your heart center. Return your focus to your heart. Be still and listen. Your heart is always in communication with you.

At the end of the day I am at peace because my intentions are
good and my heart is pure.

It makes sense If we spent our whole life studying the mind and working
on controlling our thoughts in meditation we would never get to enjoy
or live our lives. Experiencing our heart dreams is the whole reason why
we came to the earth. It's easy to get caught up in dogma and meditation
but those are only tools to help you get to the dreams in your heart.

Isn't that the whole point of life? The Heart Dream

*"The journey that never goes beyond thought is not a journey to
Awakening. Thinking is not liberation or realization. Empty ignorance.
Difference in using the teachings as practice instructions and getting
lost or stuck in concepts" ~Anonymous*

***All Heart

According to the law of attraction it is not just thought that brings manifestation, it is feeling or vibration behind the thought. And feeling does not come from the mind. I recalled the times in my life when I witnessed immediate manifestation. It happened when I cried out and demanded with all my passionate heart that I needed it done NOW. Immediately the universe responded.

One memorable moment of instant materialization came after one of my private evening yoga classes. I was in my car about to head home when my car started to make this very loud screeching noise from the front left side. My yoga students (who were men and knew a thing or two about cars) looked below my car, inside the hood and drove it around the parking lot, but couldn't figure out where it was coming from. One of them told me he'd follow me home to make sure I got home safe. It was late at night and a 45 minute drive home. I wasn't confident I was going to make it with this horrible shrieking sound. I was on the highway only about ten minutes into my journey when I lost it. I was too scared and nervous. I thought my car was going to blow up. I yelled out loud, "FAMILY. I NEED YOU NOW!!!" As soon as I yelled that declaration the sound went, Shhhoooooop, and was gone. It sounded like it was just sucked away. No more, just quiet. I couldn't believe it!!! I made it home safe.

The next day I brought my car to my mechanic. He put it up on the lift, took it apart and found nothing wrong with it. That was the first and only time it made that noise. I had no idea why that happened but I had every idea about the power of our passion, our heart, our interconnectedness and the divine help that is always at our side.

We have heard about impossible feats of strength done by humans, usually involving sacrifice and saving another for love. Where does that come from? Not the mind, it comes from the warrior heart. Your mind brings to focus what your heart is so passionate about.

When I was swimming in the annual six mile across the Great South Bay on Long Island there were times when I thought my arms would fall off because they were so tired. In my mind I imagined the scenario of my daughter on the other side in danger, what would I do? I would swim with all my might and strength to get to the other side to save her. Where does that strength and power come from? You might think your mind, but it does not. It comes from your warrior heart.

***Trust Your Gut

I got my first experience with my brave heart here in Hawaii. I was sitting on the beach with Karma people watching when I noticed a huge group of tourists pouring onto the beach. Immediately about six young adults went right into the water. I was surprised because this particular beach was not a swimming beach. It had too many rocks, a strong current and no lifeguard, with a warning sign. It's good for snorkeling on calm days, boogie boarding if you have fins, and surfing if you are experienced. I've seen so many people come out of the water all bloodied up from not knowing.

I was about to leave to grab some grinds but something in my gut told me to stay. I sat for about twenty minutes or so and watched them drift farther and farther out into the ocean until I could just see their heads bobbing up and down. I thought they must be experienced swimmers to be out that far. Then I heard, "Help, help, help!" from one of the girls.

One of the men in their group jumped into the water and brought back the girl and two others. She was crying, mascara running down her cheeks. She said they had been trying to get back to shore the whole time but they got too tired. There were still three more out there.

I jumped up, ran to my van, whipped off my dress- naked on the side of the road – didn't care- threw on my bikini, grabbed my surfboard, sprinted to the ocean and paddled out. There was no thinking involved with this decision, only praying. If I had stopped to think I would not have gone out. The waves were big, the sets were building, the current was strong, I was not an experienced surfer, and I was scared of this beach. People drowned there.

I paddled out to one of the men. He was a lifeguard from Ohio actually, but first time in the Pacific Ocean in Hawaii. He was spent! I calmed him down, put him on my board and told him we had to paddle toward shore. He responded that his arms were too tired. Having no pity, I said, "Tim, you better paddle or we're going to get crushed onto the rocks!" I swam next to him holding on to the leash. It took us a while, the current was so strong but we eventually made it.

After it was all over I sat in my van, my whole body shaking, the adrenaline was still coursing through my veins as I thought about what just happened. I couldn't believe I did that. And this is an example of what's in our divine blueprint, what's written on our hearts, the power, the strength, the courage to do something you would never do if you stopped to think. Thinking is overrated.

***What is the heart?

In school we are only taught about the heart as an organ in science class. We aren't taught about who we are and why our spiritual heart is so important.

When you say, "someone has a lot of heart," it could mean they are very dedicated or passionate. While our heart pumping 24/7 is dedication, passion is not generally ascribed to the organ in our chest. The spiritual heart holds the passion. When we transition or "die" our heart or soul, or whatever word you want to call it leaves the physical body to go on to other places. What you take with you is your spiritual heart, all the lessons you have learned, all the love you have given and received.

The spiritual heart center is the portal that houses the diamond faceted blueprint of your divine life's purpose. It is the key to everything that is YOU.

The saying, "home is in the heart," makes a lot of sense.

You are your home.

We were born to live from the frequency of the heart. The world, school, and society programmed us to live from our linear mind and our left brain.

Our ego mind was meant to be a tool for our incarnation, but the tool took over. This is our time to recognize this and to start living from the heart frequency. There is nothing we need to do, for our heart is perfect. The only thing we need to focus on is quieting the mind so the heart can lead and do the thinking. It's not easy, but it's everything. For me, what's in a person's heart is more important than their beliefs.

In *Fearless Freedom Becoming SoulFire* I talked about living from your heart. I was speaking the words and believed them to be true, but had yet to fully embrace the concept into my being and my life fully. I still struggled with the ego mind loops and living in my head. I know my head is not where the truth is, where the joy is. The mind analyzes, worries and obsesses. The heart does not do these things, the heart only feels and KNOWS.

***Unleash the Serpent

What is a serpent? Does the serpent think? Is the serpent driven by mind thoughts or the patterning of the conditioned mind? The serpent is intuitive knowing, free of thought, in touch with the divine creator within. The serpent ebbs and flows effortlessly driven by its internal instinctual knowing. It is guided by the intuitive wisdom of the divine. It just is.

This is my goal, to be like the serpent. When I catch my mind going into the loops I repeat the mantra: **Unleash the Serpent.** It helps me get control over the thoughts and return to the flow..

I am ebbing and flowing at times with the serpent's power, with the fluidity of the serpent which is free, effortless, guided by its knowing, being in its true resonance without thinking. I am able to sustain this frequency for points in time, then I slip back into the conditioned mind. This is the masculine and feminine energies that exist in all beings...the doing and the being, the giver and the receiver, the yin and yang, the right and left brain, willful intent vs fluid peace in knowing. I have mastered the masculine energy in this lifetime over and over again. I have given myself great resistance in my life experiences in order to explore and activate my inner strength. I can get through and rise above anything. I know that about me. I have an inner strength that is rock solid.

But...I am still mastering the feminine energy, the effortless allowance, free of mind loops, free of willful control. The experiences that rattle my being are signposts telling me I need to make both energetic streams, male and female/mind and heart, coalesce and meld together. Moving to Hawaii has helped me to hone in on the coalesced energy stream. Hawaii, the land where the goddess dwells, is sacred feminine energy and you learn very quickly that the flow is the only way to go.

***Shaka

The Hawaiian Shaka is a gesture that embodies the coalesced male and female/mind and heart energy. It is the traditional greeting in Hawaii you make with your hand by curling your three middle fingers while extending your thumb and little finger out loosely. It means "hang loose," "take it easy." You can't be throwing the Shaka around if you're all agro and uptight. That is not the Hawaiiana way of spreading aloha.

In an effort to "hang loose" I decided to say yes to my first invite I received when I moved to Hawaii. I was invited to go to happy hour in the middle of the day, something I never do, plus I rarely drink alcohol. I questioned the surf instructor about it being Happy Hour because it was only 1pm and he said it's always happy hour here. So I went.

Well, I wasn't enlightened in hanging loose, having a spontaneous drink in the middle of the day just made me tired and wanting to take a nap on the beach. This is how we aren't productive, I said to myself, New York fully in effect.

As I was leaving happy hour and getting into my car he asked me if I burned. I responded, "No, I tan," with a smile and left. It wasn't until months later when I realized what he was actually asking me...do I burn, herb, marijuana, bud, pot. It took me a while to get the feel for the locals and their Pigeon speak. Oh well, I'll have to find other ways to "hang loose."

So not every time I try to be like the serpent and flow with my heart energy does it lend to an amazing spiritual awakening. If the flow isn't authentic it won't lead you down your spiritual path… it might just lead you to a nap on the beach in the middle of the day.

***Message from the Council of 13 Indigenous Grandmothers

"As you move through these changing times... be easy on yourself and be easy on one another. You are at the beginning of something new. You are learning a new way of being. You will find that you are working less in the yang modes that you are used to.

You will stop working so hard at getting from point A to point B the way you have in the past, but instead, will spend more time experiencing yourself in the whole, and your place in it.

Instead of traveling to a goal out there, you will voyage deeper into yourself. Your mother's grandmother knew how to do this. Your ancestors from long ago knew how to do this. They knew the power of the feminine principle... and because you carry their DNA in your body, this wisdom and this way of being is within you.

Call on it. Call it up. Invite your ancestors in. As the yang based habits and the decaying institutions on our planet begin to crumble, look up. A breeze is stirring. Feel the sun on your wings."

***Authentic Authenticity-It Begins Within

One of the major themes in my unfolding in this lifetime is authenticity. What I am speaking has to match who I am energetically, otherwise I cannot present it. That is why book two was on hold. I hadn't yet become my own beloved, so how could I write about it? I must fully become what I speak. I must feel the awakening and become the awakening, before I put it on offer to others. If I am saying one thing but my energy speaks something else, people will feel that.

I learned that I had a lifetime where I shut down my third eye intentionally to willfully (unbalanced masculine energy) rise to the top of my career as an author and famous speaker. I presented what I thought the audience wanted to hear to receive accolades, not what was true in my heart. Now that I shined the light of consciousness on that archetype and pattern, I can change it.

Suggestions for practicing BEing: When you are in meditation or quiet contemplation, sit with your serpent, allow it to rise, feel it spiraling upward from the base of your spine, coalescing through the form and formless essence of your being. Let your serpent begin to speak to you. There is no thought involved. Your serpent will not come to life if thought is involved. The authenticity of your serpent feels different than willful mind projection. You will feel it, you will know.

***Slay the Dragon

We must slay the dragon so we can unleash the serpent.

Coming into this lifetime with an unstable mind makes life slightly more challenging! Getting control of the mind chatter is something I work on daily. What helps is starting my day with a spiritual reading- that is the medicine for my mind.

Ego thoughts replayed over and over again creates a vortex of energy around you that vibrates at a different frequency then your pure true essence – your God frequency. Our Mother Earth has the same issue, a sea of negativity that surrounds her in the psychic-astral plane that is an accumulation of humanity's distorted thought forms, destructive behavior patterns and erroneous belief systems. We are one with Gaia, so it makes the cessation of thoughts even more challenging, especially when you are so connected to the collective like me.

How do you know if they are thoughts from the ego or from the heart? Your heart or your divinity, will never give you thoughts that cause discomfort, stress or confusion. Your heart/divinity only gives thoughts that create peace, clarity and comfort. Example of a phrase of the ego mind not the awakened heart: "I have no connection to my divinity."

The ego's primary role is to separate. Our higher presence/oversoul's primary role is to unify. Ego divides, while love unites. So if you want to feel scattered and fractured, live from the ego mind; if you want to feel whole and holy, then live from the awakened heart.

If you feel like your mind is out of control now it is because it is YOU signaling you to wake up and reconnect with the divinity of your heart. At this point in our evolution the 'dragon' has gotten fiercer because of the dawning of the new earth that is here now. Fierce thoughts aren't bad, they are the signal. It is You battling you. There is no enemy except the one within. Ill fierce thoughts are the pre-programming of the conditioned mind. It is you telling you that they are no longer serving you.

There must be compatibility of the mind with the spirit.

Ego mind in control, bad. Ego mind working with the awakened heart, good! We can choose to awaken to our divinity and stay in both realities.

<u>Suggestions for practicing the art of no thought:</u> When you catch yourself in a mind loop, noticing your thoughts have gone astray or have taken control, visualize turning your thoughts off with a light switch. No judgment, just a flip of the switch. It works! You might have to flip the switch a lot in one day, but that's my little trick to quiet the mind and prevent it from taking control. Switch it off, Switch it off, switch it off. Then go back to your breath.

> "Practice the art of quieting the dragon. Slay the dragon. For the dragon is no longer serving you when you step into the light of the new reality here on earth."
> ~Archangel Michael

**Buddhist teacher: "I've never met anyone so thoughtless in my
whole life. Keep up the good work."**

Student: "Thank you master."

*** Under the White Water

There's another trick I discovered while living in Hawaii on how to find
the stillness for the mind. When I learned about my incarnation as the

Sea Maiden I was also reminded that in the depths of the ocean there is the cessation of the mind chatter. Under the water all is still, peaceful and calm. You cannot have mind chatter in the depths of the ocean's embrace. What you do have is complete presence and stillness.

In Hawaii I get to experience this first hand as I swim and frolic in the warm turquoise clear ocean of the Pacific. I also discovered something really cool and unexpected about finding stillness in the ocean. One thing you learn very quickly here on the Big Island is how to go under the waves that are about to break on you. If you don't do this, you will be tossed around like a tether ball and most likely be scraped on the lava rocks. Once you've experienced that you will never do it again!

Usually I swim out deep enough that I'm not in the ocean break, but one day I decided to stick around in the shallow water and play in the waves. One came crashing in, I ducked under and despite the frantic tumbling of the waves above me, underneath I found a bubble of complete silence, of nothingness.

You would have thought I just discovered gold! I plunged up out of the ocean with a huge smile. Wow, I thought, that was amazing. And back under I went again and again and again. It was like time stood still for a nano second under the wave and I was in a space of pure peace. I shared it with the girl next to me, but she didn't seem to partake in my same excitement. Oh well, under I went again, happy as a mermaid.

The depths of the ocean contain its own wisdom. You become one with the wisdom of the ocean when you become submerged in its womb.

I invite you to try it now…without having to actually go into the ocean.

Cup your ears with your hands sealing in the energy to hear the ocean's call. Close your eyes. Imagine you are underwater and can breathe while floating effortlessly in the ocean's embrace. Relax your shoulders. Unscrunch your face. Focus on your third eye (ajna chakra-the space between your eyebrows), take a deep breath through your nose into your belly allowing it to relax and expand for four counts, pause then exhale audibly and slowly with control though your mouth for twice as long. Pause at the end of the exhale. This is the still point of creation. Do this a few times and you will feel a space within your being of perfect stillness, calm and presence. It only takes but a minute!

The everlasting oneness of all that is and your connection to the God presence that is you is right at your fingertips. It is merely a blindfold away.

Rooted

***The SoulFire Awakening

THIS NEW MAGICAL PLACE I found under the white water wave reminds me of my signature energetic moving meditation called "The SoulFire Awakening." It helps you to discover this space of presence, the still point of creation within. The third pose of the trinity, balance pose, specifically focuses on balance between the mind and the heart and the masculine and feminine energies. When you find that space of neutrality within your body, where all is calm and perfect, even with chaos around you, you become rooted and centered in your divine power and grace.

After nine months in Hawaii I returned to my other home on Long Island- reborn again. My HB and I decided we needed a break and some space, since we were fighting so much. I went to Long Island without him. He told me to call him if I missed him and he would join me. This break was good for us, good for me. I had done so much inner work evolving in my consciousness that I needed to journey alone for a bit to integrate all the wisdom I had received.

It was during this break from Hawaii and HB while I was on Long Island that I received the SoulFire Awakening. The SoulFire Awakening are the movements that represent the words of my memoir and first book, Fearless Freedom Becoming SoulFire. Spirit said to me, "I had earned it," that I had found home in my heart and transmuted it for the masses and it was time to birth the movements that complimented the words. It is my signature energetic moving meditation. It is a brand new practice for the new light of the new earth that aligns you with your light body. Your light body is your pure essence, your true holy body. It is pure unfiltered light. It is you, the divine you.

***I Got a Feelin'

I will never forget the feeling I had in my body when I received the SoulFire Awakening moving meditation. It was completely new to me. I felt as grounded as Mother Earth, as strong as Triton and as light as the Seraphim Angels, all at the same time. It felt so good! It was such a sense of peace and security within my body and being that I had never felt before. I was reborn again. I felt more powerful and rooted and secure than I'd ever felt. I prayed it would last!

You can find all the details about the SoulFire Awakening moving meditation on Amazon in an ebook: The SoulFire Awakening

"My insides are a lot more calm thanks to the SoulFire Awakening." ~Aleeta

With the new rebirth I experienced through receiving the SoulFIre Awakening moving meditation I also received a new imprint-logo. The basis of my logos is the sunflower. The sunflower represents the totality and culmination of my BEING on earth. I came into this incarnation with the energetic template of the sunflower. The sunflower is a reflection of who I am.

The Sunflower: I am God,
a chalice of wisdom, power and love in perfect
and balanced action

The **petals** of the sunflower are my life stories and personal experiences that I bring to life by writing about them and sharing them with others. As I shed light on each experience, breathing life into the petal, its illumination becomes a blessing for others to receive within their own hearts. As the readers take the petal that most resonates with them to heal their hearts, the petals change from white to gold. In other words, you my friends, light up my petals.

The **head of the sunflower** with all the tiny seeds is for me personally. They represent my many incarnations. I am all of those seeds here and now. The sea maiden is one of those seeds within the nucleus of the sunflower, as all of my incarnations. As a multi dimensional new human I am able to ebb and flow and move around any of the seeds by focus of my breath and intention. In other words, I can bring in aspects of any of my incarnations into my being here and now by bringing my awareness and breath to any seed and it will become a part of me. It can be done freely and simultaneously with the energy of new light. It is coming into a frequency of a timestream that is alive in the grand matrix of All That Is.

I created for myself the hardships, polarity, and depths of suffering of the earth to understand and write my petals for others to heal. Now I'm stepping myself into a new energetic frequency to become the new human within the seeds of the nucleus, which is a continual work in progress.

But now, it was time to receive the final part of the sunflower: the wisdom of the **stem.**

***Da Roots, Da Root, Da Roots are on FIYA!

I used to believe having no roots and just being a free spirit gypsea roaming the world was not only cool and chic, but the way to spiritual enlightenment. With no physical baggage to tie you down, no attachments and no commitments, awakening would be a cinch. I discovered that this isn't true, at least for me. I received guidance from above that in order to create I must be rooted. How can the flower grow without the stem after all? Now that made sense!

My spirit guides acknowledged that I had found "home in my heart" but told me I also needed a physical home where I could just stay put and root. They also said that I must find sacred space alone, free of attachments and entanglements of others, including my Hawaiian Beloved. My spirit guides emphasized that it was important I create a sanctuary, a sacred space and rootedness for myself so I can mirror that energy to my HB and mirror to the masses. Energetically they will feel it from me when I am rooted in my own being and in my own sanctuary.

As you can imagine, I had some resistance to what my guides were asking me to do. Living alone was not part of my romantic fairytale. I mean, who's going to scratch my back at night? The societal programming of living together happily ever after ran deep.

After I meditated on the idea of it, I came to the conclusion that it would be the healthiest move for both of us. Shortly after this new revelation, my HB joined me in Long Island so we could spend time together. It turned out that I missed him after all. He wasn't too pleased when I told him about my new development. I tried to convey to him that we would be honoring each other's space and maybe we wouldn't fight as much and when we wanted to be together we could have sleepovers. It would be fun!

This incarnation I came to learn was not about living in the fairy tale of being in a traditional relationship or marriage – been there done that. This lifetime I came to complete my divine purpose that was not finished in another incarnation: sharing my new teachings of the divine light and new spiritual technology with the world and to heal active timelines of subservience and control in order to become independent, empowered, and free. I also wrote into my book that I would get to my Ascended Self by myself, not dependent on another.

***Free as a Butterfly

In addition to receiving the wisdom of the stem, I learned about the wings of the butterfly. Once I became rooted within my own being, I was free to fly like a butterfly. Seems contradicting at first, but when you reflect on it you will feel the wisdom in it. I had to peel away layers of the cocoon (chrysalis) to emerge into the butterfly.

A beautiful magical butterfly ready to take flight into freshness and newness that is guided by the vibrational frequency (VF for short) of my heart center, perched on my sunflower, seeping in the sweetness of my heart's dream. This was me.

***The Dark

I have been afraid of the dark my whole life. I still sleep with a night light. Recently I've come to have a new relationship with the dark. In Native American culture the dark is also known as the great VOID. It is here where there is complete stillness, emptiness, pure life waiting to be molded and created. It is a beautiful place to be. Science defines a void as a space or state completely devoid of matter, a black hole, vacuity, emptiness.

Spirituality describes darkness the same way, but takes it one step further. It is the space of No-thing, but it is here that lives the potentiality for All-things to be birthed anew, especially ourselves. This is the realm where miracles happen. It is within the void, the abyss where the Creator's Light presence is felt, seen, and witnessed as You, here and now, as the Created. You are the Creator and the Created.

***One is in the shadows to be birthed again anew.

The dark, the void, the shadows are not to be feared. This is a gift. We are empowered with this gift of being birthed again anew over and over and over. This is the gift of the SoulFire Awakening. The SoulFire Awakening offers the acceptance and ease to fold and unfold, like the sunflower unfolds her petals- into our glory and grandeur over and over again with multiple rebirthings.

Just when the caterpillar thought the world was over, it became the butterfly.

The cocoon to the butterfly
The cocoon to the butterfly
The cocoon to the butterfly

THE SOULFIRE AWAKENING REPRESENTS ALL OF OUR JOURNEYS HERE ON EARTH

STILL... THERE'S THIS

***Back to Lemuria

My HB stayed with me in Long Island for three months and we searched all over Long Island for a place for me to root. As much as I love Long Island and it will always be my home, the sacred land of Lemuria was calling me back. Plus, it was already cold and bitter in October and my tropical bones couldn't handle it.

Against direct advice provided by my spirit guides, I decided to try rooting with HB in his cabin in Puna- a lush tropical town on the Big Island. I honestly don't know what I was thinking. I can be pretty thick headed- I think they call that selective hearing. My entourage's advice was good advice, but I guess I still had some learning, living and growing to do.

***The Pueo

One day we were driving down Red Road. It is so beautiful in Puna, especially where HB lives. It's like you've stepped into another dimension, almost like a Harry Potter movie with the two hundred foot mango trees lining the one lane road on the other side is the ocean. It's just so stunning and magical.

I was observing the beautiful scenery when I thought to myself, I have heard the owl's call my whole life, yet I have never seen one in the wild. The Hawaiian word for Owl is Pueo.

Within moments of having this thought, a Pueo appeared! Mesmerized I sat watching as it flew down the road full speed with wings fully spanned out and slowly flapping in the air. It was a majestic site. I was in awe. The only thing I could do was hit my beloved on the arm and point. The Pueo came right to the windshield and then swooped toward my side of the car and flew by me making eye contact. I have come to learn when an animal makes eye contact with you they are connecting their Akash thread to yours. It's very special and meaningful. You will always be connected to them.

Wow, wow, wow. We both just sat speechless for a minute or two. It was one of those moments when words would have definitely taken away from the experience of the beautiful white snowy owl. I took in the Pueo's mighty energy with honor and thanked her for listening to my call and showing up for me. I felt so blessed and connected. It was a miraculous moment.

***Owl's Medicine- Whoo, Whoo, Whoo Are You?

In a past life I was a native medicine woman and I carried with me the knowledge that the Owl is synonymous with the gift of higher knowledge and insight. They carry the medicine of 'sight beyond illusion.' The Owl is a symbol for wisdom, because the Owl can see what others cannot, which is the essence of true wisdom. Where others are deceived, Owls see and know.

Owls are often associated with magic and witchcraft because of the nature of supernatural transformation which includes the cycles of birth and death that leads to spiritual evolution.

The snowy owl is the symbol of endurance. It represents big dreams and the ability to achieve them. It is the sign of new beginnings and moving forward in strength with all might. The Owl speaks to us about psychic ability, illumination, support, and inner knowing. It makes sense the owl came to me. Mahalo, Pueo.

"Never discourage anyone who continually makes progress, no matter how slow." ~Plato

***GPS

Even if you get direct instructions and guidance from God, you still have free will that reigns supreme. I'm very strong willed so no matter what anyone says, even God it seems, I still do what I want. It can drive me crazy because almost every time I don't listen to God's guidance, it brings about a more arduous path. It's ok if you feel like you've trodden down a road with lots of potholes, twists and turns. If you listen to your GPS-God's Positioning System-you can get right back on the path of ease and grace.

When you're on a road trip with your location GPS and make a wrong turn, the GPS never says, "Hey where have you been?" It only gives you directions on where you are going. If you take a detour or make a wrong turn it will bring you back to your original destination every time. GPS won't say, "Hey Magellan, you screwed up, now you're lost, let's turn around and just go home loser."

GPS says: "Rerouting, please proceed to the highlighted route." Having a destination, purpose or vision for your life keeps you from becoming a cork bobbing aimlessly on the ocean, observing and complaining.

Most often we can't see the big picture through our limited human perspective. We only get to see the next step. I think the PUEO was transmitting its energy of endurance to me because I had a long bumpy road ahead.

***The Jungle Life

Living off grid is not as simple and glamorous as it's portrayed in the movies. I figured out that living off grid in the jungle wasn't for me. I tried to make it work, I really gave it my all.

While we were in Long Island a mold explosion happened in my HB's car from my straw cowboy hat. It was a nightmare to get it out. The downfall to living in the jungle is that you are battling the mold constantly. It is a nearly impossible task and stressful for me being a clean neat freak. When we returned from Long Island I cleaned eight hours a day, three weeks straight, so I could get HB's cabin back to some sort of normalness and cleanliness. We ran out of water in the catchment tank, which is very unusual considering it's the rainy side of the Big Island and water is never an issue. However, we used so much of it to clean since the car, the cabin and every little thing were covered in mold from being away for three months. The well went dry.

I decided to do a rain dance in the kitchen because I really needed a shower! I prayed and danced and chanted for the rain and it came-almost immediately! As wonderful and magical and powerful as that was to call in rain from the sky, it's a lot different than walking into your bathroom, and simply turning on the faucet for a hot shower and getting water instantly. Can you imagine if each time you needed a shower you had to do a rain dance? It's a lot of work!

Besides the mold, I couldn't get used to the threat of rat lung poison from the crawly slimy snails that seemed to be everywhere. Then there were the fire ants that left burning stings for days on your private parts, centipedes, mosquitos, cockroaches or 457's to be more precise. Don't even get me started on the rats on the kitchen counter, and the spiders! I wish I was ok with creepy crawly things, but they really freak me out.

There are certain things I can give up no problem. I can live without television, radio, furniture, fancy clothes, but I learned how much I like and appreciate flushing toilets, electricity, the sun and my own money.

***Here I go again on my own...
I brought myself back to being dependent on another without consciously being aware. That whole 'letting a man take care of you' was definitely not for me. I realized this when we were shopping at the store

and wanted this particular suntan lotion and he said no. No? What? How is that? That was a wake up moment for me.

I needed to be free, in every way and that was not for me! I had lasted five weeks in the jungle, but it was time to be on my own and take my independence back. It's funny how saying something in your head to yourself is totally different from saying it out loud to another person. It wasn't easy to actually say the words to HB. I observed myself barely being able to squeak them out. I told him I needed to move back to Kona and find my own place. He asked if it was for two. I said "No, just me." That was a hard thing to say, but I had to. Finally Spirit's advice sunk in.

I moved out in December of 2019 to find my own apartment in Kona. I had nothing at the time- no money, no car, and no place to live. Luckily, I had an angel in my life who lent me enough money to buy a used minivan and that's what I lived in with Karma until I found a space in Kona.

***Amazing Gracie

My Hawaiian Beloved dropped me off at a car dealership in Kona with only my backpack and Karma. I thought to myself that I better leave here today with this minivan or I'll be sleeping on the beach tonight. I found the minivan online and knew she was the one. Six hours later I was driving off the lot in my new home. I drove her straight to the car wash and spent the day cleaning her down by the beach. I was excited but nervous at the same time. I never lived in a van before.

It turned out to be quite the experience.

Amazing Gracie, what I named my new home on wheels, had the habit of not starting sometimes and I never knew when that 'some time' would be. I would pull up to the store, go in, come out and she would be dead. There wasn't anything I could do either-it wasn't the battery. I had to remember to back into every parking space just in case I got stuck. Maybe the thoughtful gift of a brand new emergency car kit I received from one of the employees at the car dealership as I was driving off the lot was not an act of kindness, rather pity and a foreshadow!

Luckily a mechanic I knew in the area came whenever I was stranded to help me. He was a lifesaver! However, after four attempts and a few hundred dollars later trying to fix Gracie, the problem still existed.

The last time I saw him I jokingly said he was sabotaging my car so he could come rescue me. I never saw him again. I guess I hit the nail on the head. It was stressful to not know if your car was going to start once you stopped it. Drive thrus became a priority.

***Christmas in my Minivan...beep beep

Christmas 2019 was the most memorable Amazing Gracie stuck incident. Christmas Eve I had camped out in a lava field by the highway which was not very peaceful. I decided the next morning to go on an adventure with Karma and check out a new park up north. We left at 6am, stopped at a Starbucks along the way and ended up stranded.

Luckily we were stranded at a huge beautiful outdoor shopping center. At least there was food and I could shop. We ended up meeting this nice man who offered to bring us to his daughters house for Christmas dinner. The people in Hawaii are so gracious, Aloha spirit at its finest. I declined but he brought me food from the Christmas dinner anyway.

He lived close to the shopping center and I was stranded for the long run it appeared. He invited me to go paddle boarding, and I thought that I might as well take the invitation because it was better than sitting around. There was only so much shopping I wanted to do.

It was a beautiful area and a body of water that I had not been in. I was grateful for the man's kindness. In the end he even offered us an extra bedroom he had at his house. I was tempted at first. Having a nice big safe house to live in exchange for light housekeeping did sound comforting, but it felt like he was another lonely man on "Guy Island" trying to rescue me. I was done with being rescued and politely declined. I told him I didn't mind sleeping in my van. Besides, it would be peaceful since it was Christmas and no one would be in the shopping center. He towed my van to the backside of the parking lot so I could sleep in peace and made sure Amazing Gracie was under a light for safety and close enough to the stores.

I got some dinner, brought it back to my van and decided just for the heck of it I would try to start her. And just like that, Gracie started right up! I was so excited! I was going home. I could sleep somewhere I knew and felt comfortable.

I ended up going to one of my favorite spots in Kona to camp. The spot is next to the Living Stones church by the ocean. Since it was Christmas and everyone was home celebrating, I got a prime spot and hunkered in for the night. Shortly after I had settled in, a man in an SUV pulled up right next to me to camp. That made me nervous, especially since he parked so close to me. Creepy. Don't people understand about personal space!? This was before social distancing but common courtesy should have told the man to keep some distance. I went to sleep with one eye open praying to Archangel Michael to keep Karma and I safe, and my surfboard on top of my van.

Living in a minivan with this situation was really walking in faith every single step of every single day. What I found was having a routine was really important to keep my spirits up and make living out of a minivan bearable. Also, being productive was really important for me too. I knew that it was not my final destination to live in a minivan. God NO! As much as I enjoyed the new adventure, it's not something I would choose to do again. One and done.

I learned as I get older I appreciate and need certain things, like a bed, bathroom, air conditioning, French press coffee, etc. When I was in my twenties and maybe even my thirties, it was fun, but once I hit my forties and fifties, I wanted the comforts of home.

***Sanity

So every day, after I jumped in the ocean, took a shower at the beach, I would go to Starbucks for breakfast and to work on my computer looking for employment. Karma would sleep under the table and catch my crumbs. I needed to plug in my laptop because it needed a new battery so I was dependent on electricity. A simple thing like getting your battery in your Mac laptop replaced is not so simple on an Island that's in the middle of the largest ocean and requires shipping more things. While sitting at Starbucks, I thought, How hard could it be to get a job? I have a college degree, graduated with honors, have background in multiple different careers: finance, administrative, sales, health, fitness and wellness and I'm efficient, hard working, conscientious and from New York.

I looked everyday. I applied for every job, even ones I was overqualified for. I redid my resume, sent cover letters, went to a temp agency, went to an employment agency, and went in person applying for work. I applied for Nanny/babysitting jobs, I even applied for boat crew on every stinking boat in Kona. I'm CPR certified, lifeguard trained, a personal trainer, with a sunny disposition and I still couldn't get a job. I was starting to feel like something was working against me.

***Serendipity

One night I was camping at Pine Trees beach, my favorite spot to camp and met this couple with a little boy who was camping too. I immediately connected with them. It turned out the woman was a massage therapist and yoga teacher at the Four Seasons, where I had just applied online for a position. I really wanted to work there. She offered to put in a good word for me and gave me the contact of the woman to speak to for employment. I was so stoked!

I made the calls and followed up but another month went by. I started panicking. It was the middle of January, and I really needed a job yesterday.

In the meantime, I secured a place to live and moved in at the end of December. At least I had the safety and security of a house to live in. Even though it was just a room I was renting, it felt like the Taj Mahal compared to the minivan. And it was affordable. I made it my own zen space.

One night, my higher self woke me up in the middle of the night in January around 3am and put the thought in my mind to write an email to the woman at Four Seasons. I thought, *Really, now? Yup!*

So I got up, wrote her a letter, sent it and went back to sleep.

***The Letter

Dear Beth,
Happy New Year! New Decade of New Beginnings! I am stoked to be here on this sacred magical island and excited to meet with you!

I know you are super busy from what you have told me and Melissa as well; and I know things run differently here in Hawaii compared to New York. I just thought I'd send a quick note to share a few things from my heart.

It has been serendipitous that our paths have "almost" crossed. I had already been seeking employment with the Four Seasons when I met Melissa on 12/12, full moon at the beach. She told me about you and said she would pass my information along. Then two days later I received an email from Cecilia in response to my job inquiry. She also told me she would forward my resume to you since they were looking for a certified personal trainer and wellness consultant.

I was super excited and still am. For the last twenty years I had to create and recreate myself over being a self-employed single mother. I left the financial industry as a fully licensed Financial Consultant, making lots of money to follow my dreams. I became a yoga teacher and from there started my own business. I have helped and healed hundreds of people over the last twenty years. It has been the most rewarding career I have ever had. It is my divine purpose.

Last October I moved here from NY leaving my clients, students, business, friends and all I knew behind to follow my dreams, again. Not easy to do alone. It has been quite an experience, sometimes very hard, and at times I questioned my decision. I have learned so much and have grown so much.

This island has helped me to polish my rough edges. It has humbled me and taught me to dig deeper than I ever had to before, emphasizing that if I want to be a spiritual teacher and the spark in people's soul fire, I must walk my talk- 100%. I was probably at 90% before I moved here. I've come to learn, the last 10% matters.

After a tumultuous last year and a half, I have decided to stay and create a space of light and love here on this island. I haven't worked for anyone in nearly 20 years. The thought of having a boss was not one I entertained. I have never been excited to work for anyone until I found the Four Seasons. I have heard only good things about you and the company and am really excited to recreate myself again and start a new adventure and venture.

The divine feminine energy of this land has also revealed to me that I must trust and have patience, which is not my best quality I'll admit. I'm a go getter- self motivated, determined- I make things happen. This is not my first rodeo! I am fifty years young and at the peak of my career and life. However, time is running out for me. I made a choice to take a year off from my usual "work" to move here and finish writing my second book. But my resources are almost out and I will need to work very soon. I am interviewing at different places now to see what the best fit is.

I really hope to meet with you and learn more about your program and the Four Seasons. From what Melissa and others have told me, it's a great place to work.

Whatever happens, I trust in the higher path and broader perspective. I trust in Akua.

Thank you for your time Beth. Blessings on your day and I look forward to hearing from you.

With love, Soulfire
Ignite Your Soul Fire – Yoga and Wellness Services
Fearless Freedom: Becoming SoulFire – Ignite Your Soul Fire

When I woke up a couple of hours later, I was so excited to see that she had read my email and responded! She told me she would call me later and have me come in for the interview process. We really hit it off and I went through a month-long process of getting hired.

***Say What?

When I arrived for the first day of work at the Four Seasons with my first clients on February 20, 2020, I was in shock. The Four Seasons was closed!

"What do you mean? I have clients everyday here, what is happening? I need to work!" I demanded.

"No we are closed- closed because of the C," said the security guard. (Note to my readers, I refuse to add that word into my sacred sunflower, so I will refer to it as the C. But you know what I'm talking about.)

This can't be happening, I thought. But it was. It didn't seem like the universe wanted me to work after all. I had to have a serious conversation with the universe, "Ok universe, I see that getting a job is a lot harder than I thought and if this is not my path, that's fine, but at least send me some money so I can pay rent and support myself. Thank you in advance, very much."

***Ask and It Will Be Given on To You

The universe delivered. I would have never received the financial benefits that supported me for the next year and a half if I hadn't secured the job at the Four Seasons. I listened to my intuition, persisted, went the extra mile and took action. It was truly a blessing that I was so grateful for.

One of my dreams before I moved to Hawaii was to be able to spend a year off from my normal work and just focus on my writing. As a single mother, I had to work multiple jobs to make ends meet. I wanted the freedom and luxury of time to be able to develop what I was truly passionate about without the stress of paying bills.

My dream came true and it provided me with almost two years off. During that time, I developed and published the SoulFire Awakening in March 2020. In November of 2020 I created a video portal, called Living Light, on my website, which consists of over 70 videos. During the whole time I also wrote and published this book. I would have never had the time or peace of mind to do all that if I hadn't had income.

Before the money abundance came though, I had to resolve the inner conflict I was still having. I had two dilemmas now actually: One, I needed to move out already from my new Taj Mahal because my landlord became filled with fear and paranoia over the C and tried to pull me into it with her; and two, I was still entertaining the idea of lack in my consciousness.

***Entanglements...again

Moving on my own and getting my own source of income as Spirit had suggested was the path I was trying to find. I thought I was making progress but I learned living alone also means not having a controlling landlord that lives in the same house as you. She was wonderful in the beginning, we really hit it off, but then she turned paranoid about the whole "C" thing. She started accusing me and attacking me about things that weren't true. She turned off my internet which was my only means of income. She built a second door to keep people out of her part of the home and told me I wouldn't see her for months. She basically lost her shit.

I knew I had to move again to get away from her. She was another person trying to manipulate and control me and diminish my light. It was brutal for my sensitive soul. I was finally "getting" why Spirit told me to root completely solo. They have to keep reminding me of this truth since I seem to get caught in energetic entanglements of others wanting to be able to strangle my light. I'm like the prey they catch in their spider web. They are attracted to my light, want to feed off my light then I get entangled in their web of disguise, disillusion and manipulation. It is not fun.

I needed to get out and find a new home ASAP. In general, but especially during the "C" shutdown, I learned that there aren't a lot of affordable places to live on the Big Island, in the specific area I wanted to live. I was back in the struggle and the money abundance hadn't come yet because I had an internal disconnect.

Instead of being at peace with where I was at, I was fighting against it, therefore making the next step on my path impossible to create. I was back in the mind loops and the struggle thinking I had no money and needed to find a new place to live so how was that going to happen? I was still harboring the energy of lack and discontent within my heart.

It's difficult to just automatically feel abundant and free, especially if all you have known in your life is lack and struggle. This has been one of my biggest challenges. I had to redefine abundance for myself and look at abundance through a different lens. Abundance may look very different depending on the mental construct of the viewer. I had to disassemble my mental construct around abundance to better understand it.

Abundance is more than money, I realized, **abundance is freedom.** For me it's living simply and enjoying the beauty of Hawaii. I had created my dream life and had an abundance of time, the time to cook homemade meals, the time to do yoga and meditate and go to the beach. Abundance is having love in its many forms. I had to resolve the inner conflict and come to a place of peace within and surrender to my choice of where I was…this is an aspect of the divine feminine energy.

To be rich is not what you have in your bank account but what you have in your HEART.

***Balance of Masculine and Feminine Energies

While you are looking to make a change it's important, key actually, that you are at peace and ease while you are taking action. There can be no pushing against, that will produce a halt in the creation process. This is the masculine energy in an unbalanced state. Even in the crazy situation I was in I had to find a way to still be in gratitude and peace. Spirit reminded me that it's not going to fall into my lap, like I was secretly hoping it would. (Although you know there are no secrets in heaven.) I needed to be energetically reaching for it and take action so I can find my new home. It goes hand in hand. This is the masculine energy in a balanced state. Then from this place and space of peace and ease, I could make a change much easier. This was my work-finding the proper balance of feminine and masculine energies

In the meantime, even though I moved into my own space, HB and I decided to continue our relationship. The 'C' was underway and it was creating a lot of uncertainty. Neither of us wanted to be alone through whatever was coming down so HB got his own space that was right down the road from mine. It was really great at first. We tried to make it work. I was trying to stay focused on my divine mission while keeping our relationship blossoming, which was already challenging. Adding the toxic energy of my new landlord and home space made it much more stressful.

I never responded back to her in anger though, I stayed centered and calm as I held the space for peace. One day during the turmoil my HB said he was surprised I was so calm with all of M's attacks on me. I concurred. I was surprised myself! I attribute it to The SoulFire Awakening that I was practicing during this time. It really does work!

***Knuckle Up

Sometimes, however, you can practice all the spiritual shit you want, but when it comes down to it you have to take action. There's only so much of her harassment, lies and manipulation I could take. It was time to fight back.

She thought I was a naive, pushover yoga teacher. Little did she know that she would get to feel the fire from my Soul Fire! I fought back quietly, legally and smartly. I filed a police report, kept a journal of everything she did to me, hired legal counsel for free and filed a temporary restraining order. I won, which infuriated her even more.

The battle continued. She was insane enough to try to evict me during the "C" lock down. Trust me, I didn't want to live with her but I wasn't going to be tossed out on the street. I looked everyday for a new home.

I continued with the free legal counsel I had and also did my own research. She was clueless that I was such a good researcher and was flabbergasted when I served her with a big fat file of all the mandates and laws she had broken and all the fines she would be responsible for.

The court case dragged on for six months, even after I had finally moved out. The employees at the courthouse knew me by my name, I was there so often. At the last court appearance the third judge on the case asked me what I wanted to do. Apparently he was handing over the power to me instead of doing his own job. I just wanted justice. It wasn't about the money, I would have been happy if she was fined $100. It was about being responsible for her actions for the last six months, not just how she mistreated her tenant and broke the laws but lying in court accusing me of owing her money and stealing furniture. It was laughable because I'd actually improved that place and left if better then when I had arrived.

Standing in front of the judge was a pivotal moment for me. I looked over at her and actually felt sorry for her. I decided to drop the case and the charges. I was done with the energy of conflict. I just wanted her out of my energy field. Even though I was in the right, I decided to have mercy on her. I knew it was the best thing for me to do for myself, yet I still couldn't help feeling deflated.

***Trust in God

Later that night I received a phone call from a woman from an institution in Hawaii that helps people with rent. I had forgotten that I had applied a few months prior so I was surprised to receive her phone call. She told me she could get me two months rent immediately. She just needed one more document from me. I asked her why she was working at 8pm at night. She replied, "People need help." What Aloha spirit!

I was in tears. That day in court had taken a toll on my soul and this was such a blessing to receive. Was it a coincidence that the dollar amount of financial assistance I received was the same dollar amount I sued my old landlord for?

I told her I would call her right back with the information. I asked the woman's name and she replied:

"My name is Faith."
Need I say more.

God and the universe know you personally. They have your back, they see your struggles, they know your heart and they will never let you down. When you're in **PONO,** the Hawaiian word for right action, and you act kind and generous from your heart, it returns to you multiplied. My faith in humanity was restored one hundred fold that night, and the money abundance showed up immediately. Miracles abound.

***THE CHAIR 2020 = 4
A lot of my followers think I moved to Hawaii and I am living the dream life in paradise without a worry in the world. That's true to a degree, but as you can see from my stories it wasn't all rainbows and butterflies. Even with all the divine guidance I was receiving I still had bumps in the road. Waking up is a process and it takes time. The progress is that I never sank down to depths of despair like I did in the past and rebounded super quick from obstacles.

Spirit gives me a lot of visualization that really helped me to learn more quickly.

For example, they showed me a chair with the four legs grounded into mother earth. Each chair leg represented an old pattern that I needed to transmute and let go of. I did not have all the legs secured in the ground yet. I was still holding on to some old treads and patterns. The land will accept me and support me fully when I release and integrate these perceived imbalances and vibrate at a higher frequency. This was my 2020 goal.

***Healthy Boundaries

I meditated and contemplated on this guidance. I had to get the other legs in the ground to be stable and fully rooted. At least I was making progress. I had overcome my abandonment issues, now I had to figure out what old patterns and habits were no longer serving me and my highest good? I meditated, contemplated, and journaled. What we are experiencing in the outer world is always a reflection of our beliefs, no matter how much we want to blame others. I remind myself, it begins within. I knew I was reverting back to old habits and patterns, I had to resolve this once and for all!

Even though you can receive good advice and guidance doesn't mean it will be absorbed. It's good to remember when we are the ones giving guidance as well. Just because someone agrees with you doesn't mean they will take action and make the necessary change to create a new reality. Change is a process and it takes time.

For the first time I spoke up about needing alone time with my Beloved. I learned how much alone time was necessary for me, to meditate, reflect, write, grow, nurture and water my spiritual garden. I needed sacred solitude like I needed to breathe. Without alone time I was cranky and unbalanced which is what happened in the beginning of our relationship. In all of my past relationships I lost myself in the relationship but with HB I found healthy boundaries for myself and that encouraged him to have his own as well.

I'll never forget the day he thanked me for creating boundaries. Again, it's much easier to think about it in my head versus saying it aloud to him. I had just given him a talk about needing my space to create the video portal I was working on and that it could take a couple of months and it would be my priority. He told me that witnessing me following my dreams and sticking to them gave him the desire to go back to his land and work on his dreams. That made me feel good. However, maintaining harmony in our relationship was still a challenge.

Learning and Letting Go – LLG

***The Savior Complex

IT SEEMED I HAD BEEN suffering from the savior complex without consciously being aware. I was falling into the pattern of being my Hawaiian Beloved's teacher, healer and mother. Not only with my HB but other imbalanced friendships I had created here.

While "rescuing" someone is a noble act, being the "Savior" archetype is another form of not being whole within one's self. By "saving someone" you are looking externally for love. The constant need of "thank you, you saved me," fills a void, but true love for yourself can only be sourced from within you. The only one we can and are responsible to save are ourselves.

Sometimes loving someone unconditionally means walking away. You can walk away from the relationship without abandoning the person though. You can love them from a distance so you can work on your stuff and they can work on theirs, if they so choose.

***Letting Go, Sucks

Breaking up is the worst whether you are the one getting left behind or doing the leaving. I always thought it was the weirdest part of a relationship. You go from spending every day with someone, making meals, making love, planning life, having them always at your side, your best friend, and then suddenly they are not there. Gone, but not dead. Dead in a way. I don't think I'll ever get used to that.

HB is the first Beloved that I let go of. I thought being the one being left behind was heartbreaking- I felt like I had cut off one of my limbs. It was so much harder than I could have ever imagined. This was a whole new experience for me. This was the first time I was not abandoned, so it felt good to know I had done the work and healed the core limiting self belief of abandonment, yet the pain of saying goodbye to your soulmate was heart wrenching.

> **"Can you betray another to be true to yourself?"**
> *The Invitation* by Oriah Mountain Dreamer

So many times I thought of going back and rekindling our love. He only lived a mile away and I drove by his house often on my way into town. It was so hard not to stop and run to him and jump into his arms where I felt safe and loved. I didn't really want to be alone and our relationship wasn't so bad, I would say to myself. We had good times as well as bad. The temptation was great, but I knew deep down and higher up that it was time for me to rise, solo. This was my calling.

***Alone but not Lonely

It's scary to be alone, this is probably the main reason people stay together. However, being alone and being lonely are two different things. You can be alone and not be lonely if you feel complete and whole inside. If we don't come to peace and happiness within ourselves, we will not find that in a partner. You cannot give what you don't have.

I was used to being alone so I wasn't sure why this time it was hard to let go. For as much as we had our challenges, we also had our flow and fun. We were best friends and we pretty much loved to do the same things. He was always up for my spontaneous adventures! He played music and I loved to dance. He was a water man and I was the sea maiden. And he always walked Karma with me, which is something I loved and cherished about him. He also didn't get jealous over the attention I gave her.

I realized how much I enjoy being in a relationship and having someone at my side. He gave me that gift. I used to tell myself I didn't mind being alone and could grow old alone. That was a lie I told myself to protect myself from getting rejected. No one wants to be alone. I don't care who you are or what you have convinced yourself of. It's only a protection mechanism for your heart. Being alone for a period of time to heal and reflect is natural and necessary but not forever.

The true dream in my heart, like many of us have, is to be in a healthy harmonious partnership with someone who will grow with you, knows you, understands you, sees you fully and completely for who you are and loves you anyway…warts and all. Bonding is in our biology after all.

***It's OK

The day I realized he had moved out of his place in Kona shook me to the core. It brought me comfort to drive by his house and know he was still there. I was on my usual drive into town when I noticed the OM tapestry I had given him was no longer hanging from the front window. My heart sank. I turned around at the top of the hill to drive past his house again just to make sure. His place was empty. I felt sick to my stomach. I told myself to breathe, that everything would be ok. As I was driving away a car drove past me with the license plate, "It's OK." God and our angels comfort us in a thousand ways. Thank you Akua.

You are never alone, beloved.

***The Ascension Dream

Wisdom, clarity and direction come to me in my dreams and my dreams get right to the point. About a month into my break up with HB I had a dream on the night of the full moon lunar eclipse. In my dream we lived together. I was going back to our apartment but to get in you had to climb a tall ladder. I was at the top of the ladder with only two more steps to go, but I was frozen, my fear of heights had kicked in. I was so scared.

Gripping the ladder, I carefully turned my head and eyes to look down. There were a lot of people walking around below me, attending to their business, so no one noticed me. I yelled out to HB, "G..., G..., G...," but he wasn't there. I felt heartbroken that he wasn't there for me.

I turned my head back in time to watch the screws at the top of the ladder pop out and fall off. The ladder was just leaning on to the ledge because of balance and nothing else. Paralyzed in fear I screamed "HELP!" and a rush of people came toward the ladder to help me. Then I woke up.

The ladder is symbolic of Ascension. Ascension is about evolving in our God consciousness, remembering our divinity and returning back to the higher dimensions of living in oneness and unity. Ascension has been my main focus and my divine life purpose.

Like I said, I'm going to ascend solo. I wrote in my book of life that to become my God Self I had to do it by myself, not relying on or depending on another to raise me up. Ascension was something I must do on my own.

The people saving me on the ladder was the same message I received from the face reader in Nepal. The ladder dream made total sense to me and was a confirmation of what I already knew. I will always be loved by the people.

***Compassionate Action

All the next day I felt angst in my gut from the ladder dream. So many feelings came up during the course of the day: guilt, sadness, longing, fear, anger, righteousness, love. I reminded myself how could he be there for me when he can't show up for himself? I knew he was hurting too and going through a lot. He was struggling with health issues on top of a broken heart. I knew exactly how that felt.

I went to bed praying for him to be comforted by his angels, to help him heal and find the light. It was a reminder that we have the power to change ourselves and the world with compassionate action.

I do not actually have to see him or speak with him to communicate with him. Sometimes that only brings more frustration and hurt if one or both people are not ready for in person interactions. But I can always take compassionate action by going into my heart and higher self and connect to his higher self and sincerely wish for his healing, for the light to be shown to him and for his path be made with ease and grace.

It's ok to be sad and to miss him, I reminded myself. If I didn't miss him then that would mean I really didn't have a deep or meaningful connection with him. That thought shifts my sadness to a higher perspective. I allow and embrace the higher perspective instead of trying to ignore or shove the feelings of sadness down somewhere or make it go away. I will never stop loving him.

A helpful acronym for this type of emotional transformation:
ROAR
RISE OBSERVE ACCEPT RELEASE

***Mirror mirror on the wall, who's the fairest of them all?

Relationships are mirrors and they can be our best teachers if we allow them to be. They are triggers to look deep within to see where the wounded aspects of our being are to be seen, felt and integrated back to unity and wholeness. We are feeling the discomfort for no other purpose than to heal it. When I talk about relationships it can be any form of relationship, but the most intimate ones are usually the ones that bring us on the fast track of healing.

In the beginning my HB and I were perfect mirrors. We had pretty much the same insecurities, triggers and reactions. I used to think we were brother and sister because we were so similar (and I'm sure we were in one of our lifetimes together!) I felt like I was talking to myself sometimes when I talked with him.

But once you are not at the same energetic vibrational frequency the relationship must change. If one person is doing the inner work and changing their reflection in the mirror and the other remains stagnant then it's difficult to stay together because you are no longer energetic matches. I never stopped working on myself during our relationship, no matter what was happening around us: break ups, turmoil, TRO's, pandemics,complete crumbling of the old world. I kept doing the inner work: reflecting, self contemplating, meditating, healing my wounds, changing my reactions, creating, and following my divine destiny.

It seemed we were no longer mirrors. And it wasn't that I was perfect, far from it, but I had already put in seventeen years of working on myself, and I still continued to make that my priority. Our lives were very different. While I was working on healing my inner Self, he was focused on raising a family.

***Progress:)

My HB and I were at Starbucks getting coffee and one of the employees spoke to us with a "TUDE" when we asked for sugar. I didn't let it affect me because I had been feeling so high and happy and said to myself, She must be having a bad day, it's ok, and let it go. My HB had the opposite reaction. When we got into the car he expressed his anger toward her and it put him in a bad mood. I tried to share some of my thoughts and experience about managing emotions and not letting others impact your mood, but he was not open to listening. I get it though. If this Starbucks trip had happened a few years prior I might not have had the same calm reaction.

When we can walk the planet in this state of being, instead of letting other people's moods and energy affect us, we are in the state of mastery. Controlling our emotions and reactions is part of the mastery, but the true mastery is to not be triggered to begin with. This is a work in progress for me still, but the triggers have lessened. Triggers aren't a thing when you can remain in the place within your being that feels whole and content and peaceful.

***Who's in this Relationship?

Soulmate relationships are designed to show us where our wounds are by triggering them in each other. I like Dr. Bruce Lipton's explanation of relationships when he says that there are actually four in a relationship: your conscious, your subconscious, their conscious and their subconscious.

The conscious mind, connected with our divine source and spirituality, is the creative mind that expresses our desires. In contrast, the subconscious mind is a hard drive of programmed instincts, experiences and acquired habits, whether good or bad. We live 90% of our lives by our subconscious mind. The only way to access the conscious mind is to be present, to be in the NOW moment.

That is why affirmations and mantras don't work for people that haven't 'updated' their subconscious mind by deleting old files or erroneous beliefs. The subconscious mind is just like a computer. When the storage is too full, you need to clean it out and reboot.

In an "ideal" partnership both beings would be awake and aware. Both would be working on their "shadow" and able to communicate rationally with the other to help each other work through the wounds from their higher selves/perspectives. If both are asleep the drama can be never ending because no internal work is getting done by either. If only one is awake and working on themselves the relationship becomes unbalanced. The only sane thing to do is leave the relationship, continue to work on yourself, heal and hold space for the other to rise into their glory and divinity. If you don't do this from a distance the pattern will never change.

"The disparity that this world offers you is the emancipation from shadow into the light. Each and every time you strengthen the palpable muscle of reflection you move inward into the space of your True Self's knowing, that you are the wielder of your chosen experience, delicately and intricately choosing to lead you upon your path of illumination that was ordained and written by the You that is pure, unfiltered, holy and free."~ Jonas and May Channeled via Dana Livoti Sita

> **"The disparity that this world offers you is the emancipation from shadow into the light."**

***Your Journey is Perfect

We're all growing and learning and awakening at different rates and times. You cannot force someone to awaken when you are. The other being within the relationship has free will and their own destined time frame to unfold their shadow. Before we came down to earth, we all chose what we wanted to work on during the incarnation. Some souls choose to not go through the process of healing and purification. It could be because of fear or because of clinging on to the old energy and paradigm or because they are deeply stuck in the lower frequency energy. Most of the collective is choosing to stay in what they feel is familiar. However, refusing to let go of pain and suffering keeps you in stagnation and stagnation is death to the soul.

We are living in the time of the Great Awakening – The Golden Age – The Aquarian Age. It's a momentous time that has been prophesied by the indigenous people for centuries. As the lifting of the veil happens and we ascend into 5D, no one can piggyback another soul into the higher state. One can show the way – but one cannot go through the purification and healing process for another soul.

***3D Drama: "You spot it, you got it."

Sometimes what occurs when a strong stubborn soul has forgotten who they are is denial, deflection and projection. If they haven't been doing the deep inner work on themselves, the unhealthy part of the ego or pride will fight so hard to stay intact that they will deny and deflect anything pointing toward them i.e,. not take responsibility for their part in the relationship. Usually what comes after is an unbridling of their wounds or unresolved shadow on to you, i.e., projection.

Carl Jung says it best: "The psychological rule says that when an inner situation is not made conscious, it happens outside, as fate. That is to say, when the individual remains undivided and does not become conscious of his inner contradictions, the world must perforce act out the conflict and be torn into opposite halves."

Energetic muck is real. When you are left holding their share of unresolved energy it's very draining emotionally because you carry it until you address it. For me emotional drama is much more debilitating than physical. I'd much rather train for an ironman than to go on the emotional rollercoaster of deflection and projection. Been there, done that. New chapter.

One night about seven years before I moved to Hawaii, I was sitting relaxing at home in Long Island when I heard a pounding on my door. It was one of my housemates/acquaintances who was intoxicated and decided to unload her anger and vile toxic energy out on me. I was shocked because I just did her a huge favor and helped her cat who was left outside in the storm. I reacted by calling her the "C" word (first time I did that), gave her the finger, slammed the door in her face, stomped up the stairs and sat on the couch to process what the hell just happened.

Within a few minutes this nausea came over me strong and hard. I ran to the bathroom and hung my head over the toilet. I was so sick to my stomach so suddenly. I never get sick so it was hard for me to handle it.

I prayed to Archangel Raphael to take it away from me because it was not mine. After I threw up a few times, it was out of me and I was 100% better. I had literally thrown up the toxic waste that she dumped on me. As much as it sucked to feel so sick to my stomach, I was relieved I processed her dark negative energy so quickly and didn't keep it in.

When someone lays their toxic crap on you and you can feel it lingering there are many different tools and methods to clear it from your energy field. It doesn't have to be as extreme as throwing up. My favorite method is sitting in nature, breathing deeply and recalibrating yourself to the light frequency of nature. Salt water is another great purifier. If you don't have the ocean available you can take a salt bath. Sage is great, but some people don't like the smell. And you can always breathe deeply and ask your higher self and guides to help you release stagnant dark energy that is not yours. I offer other methods on my video portal, **Living Light,** that can be helpful.

***Don't take it personally, actually don't take anything personally

I'm getting so good at sniffing out projection now. In 2017 I lost two of my closest dear friends. It was a shock. Over the last five years the people that have been closest to me in my life just dumped and jumped. Sometimes a great purge is necessary, but it doesn't mean it doesn't hurt.

As you are leveling up and rising into new energetic vibrational frequencies it is common that friends and soulmates will try to keep you down. Most of the time they are not doing it consciously. It's an insecurity within them to keep you at their level. This is quite normal and good to be aware of. Don't second guess yourself like I did. Another pattern I worked on breaking.

I use this as fuel to be even more firm in my conviction and resolve of who I am and where I am going. I know the work I've done to get to where I am today, the sacrifices I've had to make, and no one, no one is going to take that away from me. Naysayers try to plant seeds of doubt in your mind but your heart knows. Your heart always knows.

Once you've experienced that lifting into the light, into a new perception, a feeling of true joy and peace, you will not wish to ever sink back into the quagmire of the old earth and old 3D again. That means you might have to cut ties with "friends" that are not in the same energetic frequency as you. This is something I had to do during the creation of this sunflower, but you must protect yourself from energy vampires. They are real. The challenge here is to maintain that exceedingly high frequency energy and to grow ever higher and higher into the truth of your Soul-challenging to say the least in this current day and age when the old world is falling apart and most of the people you've cared for are falling with it.

*** Circle Back

In *Fearless Freedom Becoming SoulFire*, I healed my core issue: abandonment. However, I wasn't entirely in the light of my being, I still had one toe in the dark. This core limiting belief of finding love and security outside of myself was still hanging around and it was why I brought HB into my life.

Break up trauma doesn't go away overnight with one break up or relationship. It's not a one and done. You encircle it and encircle it, each time you encircle it you unthread a different piece of the trauma little by little, and the layers begin to heal until you are clear and free. It's like untangling a big knot. You have to start on the outside with the easier threads to unweave, then eventually layer by layer the knot untangles.

The wounds or karma from relationships can run deep through many timelines and generations. When you heal a deep wound like this you are not only healing it for yourself but for the collective, and energetically that can be exhausting!

Sometimes we circle back with the same soul and sometimes we circle back with a new soul re-living the same karmic pattern. And sometimes we circle back lifetime after lifetime. On this dense planet where souls forget who they are and why they decided to incarnate, many forget their soul contracts, and allow themselves to be veered off their path. When this happens, the soul then finds a lifetime in which they added more soul lessons to be mastered, than actually master them. Make no mistake, you will keep repeating lessons until it's healed and fully integrated. This is your soul's purpose.

The destiny of man (humanity) is to awaken from spiritual amnesia and to realign with the original intention of their soul.

I circled back with my Hawaiian Beloved many times; like going through a car wash back around and around. I learned not to judge myself or my journey and to have compassion and kindness for myself and for him. It was not an easy wound to heal and it was a biggie. Becoming the Beloved within runs deep and through the collective of almost every soul on the planet.

"There's no coming to consciousness without pain."~ CG Jung

***Shower Wisdom

"I love him," I said to myself in the shower as I did my daily thinking and my daily missing of my Hawaiian Beloved. This time I heard a response back from deep within the recesses of my being, "But I love myself more." And there it is.

Soulmates are special, they come with extra attachments. Even though deep down you know it's the right thing for your soul, it's still very hard to let go. It takes a brave soul to step out of the karmic pattern of familiarity to go into the unknown alone. But sometimes loving yourself means saying NO.

NO MORE.

When you think one thing, feel another and do something else, you are being dishonest with yourself and that's the ultimate betrayal. When you say yes when you really want to say no, you create negativity. Negativity is knowing in your gut that something or someone isn't right for you and doing it or staying with them anyway. This causes inner conflict, which in turn can cause imbalance, illness and disease because you are cutting off your life force energy by not being in your truth. I was getting 'blows to the gut,' and still tried to make it work with HB. When you do that to yourself or allow another to do that to you, you are cutting off your own life force energy and not being in your power. You are not being you, which is being in suffering because being you is love.

The fear of not having a partnership, no companion, being alone and being lonely brought me back to him every time. It's not them however, it's a fear of not being whole within yourself. This is one of the scariest things, but there is no one, no thing that is going to fulfill your wholeness but your connection to God, and to your God self within.

Everyone wants to feel complete and whole with a union of some sort, but first we must master that energy and realize that wholeness is only truly found within you. When you can sit with the energy of wholeness coming from within and feel it and become at peace with it and say to yourself, "Yes, I am whole, I am divine," and fully feel the space of neutrality within your physical body and know you don't need another, you have arrived. When you are whole, then a truly divine partnership can come into your life. The universe will orchestrate on your behalf and bring you the perfect vibratory match.

KNOWLEDGE IS A RUMOR UNTIL IT LIVES IN THE BODY

***Cognize it
In order for spiritual transformation to occur and last it has to take place in the physical. That is why we chose a human body, so we can actually create and experience the change in the physical/tangible. And that requires action to make change.

Let's use swimming for example. You can't learn how to swim by reading a book. Even if you read hundreds of books to learn how to swim, you will not KNOW for sure that you can swim until you get in the water and try. Words don't teach, experience does. That is why self-help books, while helpful in planting seeds, don't actually make change. Change comes from effort and experience.

When you practice swimming, you understand that you must exert effort. I remember the first time I did half a lap across the pool in my first swim lesson. I clang to the side of the pool panting like I was going to die. Then after a few weeks of practice I was warming up with 500 meters (20 laps) like it was nothing. Once you get a feel for it, the effort is gone, and you can swim with ease. It will become a part of you once you grasp it and something you will never forget.

This is the same for anything we are learning, whether it's evolving in our consciousness or spiritual powers, learning a musical instrument, or a sport, change in lifestyle or habits...there is no way to absorb it until we physically practice it.

"You are what you do, not what you say you'll do."~CG Jung

***Quantum Forgiveness

Our divine sacred union was the catalyst for me to step into the frequency of 5D and live it. I had evolved so much that I was at the pinnacle point. We are divine sacred catalytic soulmate partnerships. We stuck it out together. He was the main player in my healing of these wounds.

At first, I had a misperception of who he was- the knight in shining armor coming to save me when he was the catalyst who was the holy light to help me transform and alchemize the old karmic threads of subservient energy and rise into the Soulfire that I am.

He was the rock because he stayed and allowed me to heal. He served me. Here I am again to push this button and this button- that's divine sacred holy relationship. He signed on to do that for me in this lifetime. How beautiful.

Instead of getting angry and holding on to bitterness for how much his actions hurt me in the end for he did exactly what I specifically asked him not to do, I choose to thank him. If he didn't do the things he did to make me feel so much discomfort and pain, I would have never left. And that's how we forgive and rise. With this perspective there is actually nothing to forgive, more like gratitude to the soul for his role in my BEcoming.

When you can change your perspective and reframe a relationship and look at them in this way, you heal yourself, each other and the world. AHO.

Sometimes the soul that does you the greatest harm is the highest service and an act of love.

***Everything is Energy, Even People

What I found helps to ease the pain of breakup is when we take the person out of the equation. It's an **energy** that you're playing it out with. You're trying to shine a beacon of light on that energy to transform and rise, but that energy is choosing to stay stagnant and veiling themselves, cutting themselves off from their divine light and oversoul which is love. That energy is choosing that, choosing to put the veil on. All you can do is turn your back on suffering and hold space for them to heal. You cannot make someone change and you cannot rob someone of their journey.

***Turn Your Back on Suffering! ~All the Angels

When you are in suffering, you are not loving yourself because what is suffering? Suffering is the absence of love, the absence of the knowing of what it is that you are: pure unfiltered holy love of God. God is nothing but pure positive energy, love and light. When you are in suffering it simply means you have temporarily forgotten who you are.

Pain is inescapable in the 3D world of illusion and forgetting, but suffering is up to the individual. Suffering is self inflicted. You are the creator and participant in your own wheel of suffering through control, which is masquerading as fear. Suffering is the repetitive incessant desire to repeat cycles of disempowerment and separation that masquerade as control, fear, anger, hatred, jealousy, illness, ego will. It's your choice.

Pain is inevitable. Suffering is optional.

And fear, the polar opposite of love, is the root of all suffering. The true essence of fear is the veiled heart, the veiled heart that is unable to feel their own inherent light. So when we close our hearts, we are closing ourselves down to the light and love that we are, and we suffer.

> "Fear comes from the wrong belief that you are separate from the One Source, that you are not whole, holy and complete as is. It is the forgetting of who you truly are...the holy breath of God incarnate." ~Quan Yin

Many beings stay in suffering because it's their comfort zone-it's what they are familiar with. You can either focus on the passion or focus on the resurrection. What do you think Jesus wanted us to do? His message was about the resurrection but somehow the most painted image in the world is the passion – Jesus hanging on the cross. No wonder why the world is programmed to be in the suffering.

Time for an upgrade, a new paradigm and a new world,
starting with us.
We are the love we've been looking for.

***"Don't go back to sleep" -Rumi

It was time. I circled back many times not only in this relationship but to all my relationships to heal layer after layer of wounds and traumas. Now it was time to circle back one last time and to finally be whole within myself. This was the last "purification of this wound."

Don't go back now, I said to myself. I had no choice with my team of angels and spirit guides behind me huddled together shoulder to shoulder pushing me forward, not letting me turn around. "You go girl, don't turn back," they chanted. I had to allow myself the space of freedom to finally fully heal this last trauma. I spoke with my future self who is saying to me, "I'm over here on the beach in my white dress looking into the eyes of my true reflection."

My true reflection is a reflection of the beloved that I know that I am embodying. I can only become that future me by embodying my heart's light of being my own Beloved. Dramatic pause. Breath.

***Summary...Only the soul can create change

It's always the first step and the seed that is planted. You hear the statement: "You are your own Beloved." You wonder, what does that mean? (I heard it but ignored it basically.)

No one ever fully knows what that fully means until they start uncovering and healing all the traumas. It's not just one snip of the scissor, I went through the healing over and over again and unthreaded each and every last of the entangled knot.

Healing doesn't happen like this: You hear it once or twice or multiple times and then you heal it. No, you hear it, you understand it and then the person comes to be the mirror to actually heal it by being the catalyst, over and over again. You have to go through it, through the fire, to burn away all that is not Godly then feel the peace within your body.

Then and only then could I step into the space of my future self, solo, cutting the entanglements. It's the hardest thing, but I did it. Once you've gone through this alchemical fire, no one or no thing can ever take that away from you. You've gained your true sovereignty, you've become fortitude in fluid form.

***Lilith

Let's go quantum here: when you vibrate and be at true peace with it, if you can imagine it mentally and feel it in your heart it's because it has happened already -it already is. Therefore, it will happen, it's you tapping into your future self. It's a timestream in the grand matrix of all timestreams.

One day during my separation from my HB and feeling sadness I was woken up from a nap by a woman's voice. She called out to me, "Lilith." It was a loud and clear voice. When I shared this with Sita, she responded back with this:

Lilith,

I am feeling like she is your guide right now. Another aspect of you on a different timeline. She is fierce with her conviction. Strong with her message of purity and rooted in her sovereignty. She is the flame of the crimson heart. She has come to walk you through the gateways of your next rebirth. She is fortitude in fluid form.

I know her. I feel her. I feel Lilith. She is me. She is my guide right now, another one joining my entourage. I love Lilith and am grateful for her presence. I need her!

As I stand rooted in my sovereign freedom, it frees him to FEEL something new and opens spaces and places within his being to heal. As I become whole I offer him the space to rise. The energy was not serving me anymore. That doesn't mean his energy cannot shift, he has free will. I hold space.

This is the prescription.

When we stop looking for someone to complete us, we find completion in ourselves. The purpose of relationship is not to have another who might complete you, but to have another with whom you might share your completeness. AHO.

By talking about my own life and relating it to others I'm paving the way for others to walk the way of grace. ~God

ANOTHER GATEWAY TO BEING YOUR OWN BELOVED – BYOB

***Selfie Love

Finding home in your heart is a gateway to becoming your own beloved. I also discovered that self-love is also a gateway. I developed more solid self-love through my relationship with HB, however, self-love is not the same as being your own beloved. It is a gateway to the beloved within. When you say that you love yourself, which self are you referring to? Self love pertains to your form, to the human part of you. Being your own beloved pertains to the formless, the holy essence that you are. It is different.

In our society we are focused, maybe even obsessed, with the physical. I don't judge people who want to look good and stay in shape, heck I'm one of them. It's natural to want to look good, but there needs to be a balance between loving the physical body and loving the Self.

***BBL

Have you heard of the Brazilian Butt Lift? Not to be mistaken with the BBL procedure that costs thousands of dollars or the Brazilian bikini wax. The Brazilian Butt Lift is an at home workout using ankle weights and exercise bands. The premise behind selling this program was that if you put a pencil under your butt cheek and it didn't fall that you needed to lift your saggy ass bum! And there was no better way to do it than with the Brazilian butt lift program.

Well, I did the pencil test and failed. So of course I was hooked and bought the program. I followed the exercises at home everyday for weeks. And while it definitely made my derriere more firm, that stinkin pencil never dropped. This was during my triathlon days so I was in great shape before I started the program. After years (yes years!) I came to the conclusion that my body shape, specifically my keister, was the way it was and if I ever put a pencil under my cheek and it stayed there that was because I was suffering from rigor mortis. How much more self torture must I subject myself to, right?

If all we do and focus on is our form we will never find true peace, happiness and freedom within. We will always be a slave to the ego mind and the physical body. What defines us is knowing who we are – divine eternal infinite holy light, not our physical body. We have a body, we are not our body. That distinction is important to know. Our physical body will change, droop in all the wrong places, sag, wrinkle, gray. Next thing you know you have extra hair growing out of your ears and nose but not your head, and weird bumps and growths showing up in weird places.

I contemplated getting botox, a lot of my close friends do it and they look great. But I decided I would do Godtox instead. After all, aging is a human process and I'm God's Divine Source Energy having a human experience, so I think it will work.

***The Formless

The idea of loving yourself points to the essence of "form," the physical self. Sadly a lot of people don't even get to this point in their development. Self love is an act of human doing in 3D space and time and we need to do it because part of us is human with an ego mind and body. Being your own beloved is a vibrational frequency, it is an energy or resonance. It is not a doing. Being your own beloved is the formless space of the I AM presence. It is experiencing yourself as that- the space of no thing and all thing. It is infinity, All That Is. It is you. It is God. It is Love. You are all that and a bag of chips.

Being your own beloved is being in perfect harmony with your inner true resonance, the knowing, the embodiment of your Be-ingness. It is the space where you seek nothing No-thing other than your essence of Be-ing. It is the peace, the stillness within…It is home.

Like I said in the introduction, we cannot be our own beloved if we don't know who we are. Now you understand why remembering who you are is so dang important!

"However learned, rich or powerful he may be, if a man has no clear knowledge of what he really is, all his learning, greatness and power are merely fictitious! Hence, the first lesson to be learnt is about one's own Self."

God

***Seeing the Higher Truth Beyond the Matrix

SOME PEOPLE DIE AND COME back to life, what is known as a Near Death Experience (NDE), to gain spiritual insight and truth. I didn't have to have an NDE to gain spiritual truth. I had a 'prophetic vision' – outer body experience in my backyard during a dark time and the writing of my first book, Fearless Freedom. It was one of those multi dimensional experiences where words can't really describe the depths and profundity of it, but I will try regardless.

I was standing outside in my yard walking Karma when instantly I was out of my body looking down on the earth and all of humanity. It was like a sunroof opened and I was peering down through it seeing what God sees with omni present vision and awareness. I saw all of humanity at one time with a veil covering their heads and the front of their faces. The Humans appeared like they were all walking around asleep, blinded to their true nature. They had no idea of the divine within and of their connection to God, that they were God. They were walking sleepers.

Then I felt this huge wave of emotion come over me, I gasped, and was right back down in my body. The universe was giving me a glimpse beyond the maya-matrix into the higher reality of truth.

I stood there for a few minutes taking it in, not believing what just transpired. I saw it, I felt it. It was profound. In that instant I saw the core problem of the entire world: the forgetting of who we are. We are the omnipresent energy of the Almighty Creator. We are God expressing itself in this physical vessel.

***All Is God

Einstein said, "God is all that exists, it is the sum of all energy in the universe." Consciousness equals God. The words are interchangeable.

Teaching by Michael Love/Pleadians:

1. Consciousness is the primary existence
2. You are this consciousness
3. There is only one consciousness in the universe

"I am God" doesn't give you a God complex. "Have I not said, you are all the same as well." This is the correct teaching about who God is. Every being in the universe is God Source, is an emanation of the same one consciousness that exists. Every saint and sinner is God.

ALL THINGS ARE GOD MANIFESTED
ALL BEINGS ARE GOD MANIFESTED
THERE IS NOTHING THAT IS NOT GOD
IT IS IMPOSSIBLE FOR A THING NOT TO BE THIS

What is called God is the whole of the universe and trying to place something outside of that whole produces error.

YOU ARE GOD, SO GET OVER IT.

When you are truly resonating in the vibrational frequency of your I Am Presence there's no more loving yourself because you are love itself. It's like asking the water to be wet or asking God to love him/herself. God is omnipresent love.

The song by the Beatles, All You Need Is Love, is another way to keep us trapped in the conditioned mind and form looking for love externally.

You don't need love, you are love.

***Let Go and Let God, Within

The mantra: "Let go and let God" is a healing balm for my soul. It's helpful especially when you are a controlling person, like me. When I say the words I can feel the tension leave my body and mind. And why wouldn't it? I'm giving my problems up to a higher power, God and the universe and that's a big relief.

I had a shift in awareness about this statement one day during meditation. I was repeating the mantra to myself and realized that the God that I'm letting it go to is me, the God within me. I am that God. So a more accurate statement would be then: "Let go and let God within me."

We take back our power when we come to fully know and be the "Let Go and Let God Within."

So many people are relying on the big guy in the sky to fix their problems and the problems of the world. And that's just not how it works. When we let go and let God within we take responsibility for our lives. My opinion is that religion, while it can have many beautiful and truthful aspects to it, keeps us separate and divided within and without. We came here to learn responsible co-creation as spiritual/human beings. When you leave your life to an outside force, even if it's God, you are still disempowering yourself.

If you think confession is going to save you, think again! You don't need forgiveness from God, God is not a judging God. You need forgiveness from yourself. That will set you free. And if you believe God is responsible for the problems in the world, you are mistaken. We have free will. That is our divine gift and our birthright when we came here to earth. God is not controlling us and making the mess. We are. All the pain and suffering in the world is due to our human mis-creations and we are the ones that have to be responsible to clean it up.

The way to the future is not an externalness but an internalness. We need to activate the internal compass and call upon the source inside, not the source that sits in the sky. We came into these bodies and to the planet with God inside, with the Creator inside. When the God inside became the God outside we didn't just remove God from inside the society, we removed God from ourselves. It's a disservice and a dysfunction to the entire body of humanity.

***I Created the Rainbows???

Yes Beloved," they say with a sigh, "You created the rainbows."

I'm not saying there is no God outside of us, because I do believe in a personal external God/Goddess or God parents. I believe in guardian angels, spirit guides, light beings, ascended masters, our star family…but we are also part of Source Energy. In the higher reality there is no difference giving it up to a God outside of yourself and giving it up to God within because we are ONE. But on a human level of understanding there is a big difference.

I used to walk around asking for "signs" constantly. I'd say to God, "If I should do this, show me a sign." I would get them almost all the time, but it wasn't until this recent spiritual awakening that I realized that it was me, My God Self, giving me the signs.

All the rainbows I created! What a revelation. Take it one step further, the books that resonate deeply with me – I wrote them, in another time-line as a signpost for me to remember and wake up now.

You know you've reached another level of spiritual awakening, when you say to yourself, You can't make this shit up, then you catch yourself and say, Oh yea, I did.

My spirit entourage have a sense of humor like mine. Once I was told that they mirror us even with their humor. After I asked them if it was me creating the rainbows they offered a name for one of my books. They sighed, rolled their eyes and said "'OG I Really Am the Creator,' would be a good name for your next sunflower, Beloved."

I can't tell you how many times Sita said to me, "But you are God brother. You are God." I can literally hear her voice in my head. And I'm like, "Yea, yea." Not taking it in fully. I only intellectually understood it. It wasn't until it seeped into my being and my heart felt it, that I had the true awakening. "Holy shit! I am God!!!" The light bulb went off.

Now when I hear someone say "Let go and let God," or "God has a bigger plan for me," or "Trust in God," in my head I say: The God within. It's just for my own way of cementing and cognizing it so the change can stick. This is important practice. When I used to attend Catholic Church services and we had to repeat the verses like a parrot I never would say, "I am not worthy." To me that was complete bullshit. What kind of religion indoctrinates you to be unworthy. Words are living energy and part of the cycle of creation. Be mindful of the words that you cut the air with. Words are creation.

***Within

During my first adventure to the Big Island to visit my daughter, before I actually moved permanently to the Big Island, I delivered this message to myself.

I took the day and rented a car to go exploring solo. I found this beautiful park, sat by the water's edge and talked to God, making my usual requests. I even gave God my Christmas list. I told God that I had been a good girl and that I earned it and deserved it, "So please can you make my life easy and just deliver my Christmas wishes?" I could just see God rolling her eyes at me. But instead she gave me a big sign that I couldn't miss. As I left the park a car pulled in front of me that had a license plate that read, **WITHIN.**

Now I was the one rolling my eyes! I know, I know, I know. I just thought maybe for once life could be a little easier. I was still one toe in the looking for answers and manifestations outside of myself.

After the unmistakable message I returned home to New York and made a vision board on January 1, 2018. The vision board was all of the Big Island. "Get me there asap," I prayed to the universe. Exactly nine months later, on October 1, 2018, I was on an airplane flying across the country to live in Hawaii. I was not consciously planning that the date would be exactly 9 months...to rebirth... HHHMMMM

BEGIN TO SEE YOUR WORLD THROUGH THE EYES OF SOURCE THE EYES OF WHO YOU REALLY ARE.

I had another major shift during my cocooning. I realized that if I am God then I can choose to look at the world from this awareness, meaning that the me that's looking out from behind my physical eyeballs can be my God self, or I can look out from behind my physical eyeballs from my human self. It's all up to me. But what I choose is everything.

When we look through the eyes of our human perspective we are limited to what we can see. Our vision will be tainted and influenced by what is programmed in our subconscious aka our belief system. We've all been programmed so there is no shame in admitting this. If you believe in lack you will see lack. But that is not the higher perspective and the real Truth.

If I look at life and my world through the eyes of Source, through my God eyes, I only see abundance, beauty, joy, perfection. Even if what's appearing before me has contrast or perceived negativity, it can still be seen as perfection. It's a perfect signpost for me to get back on path to my divine purpose.

This is a huge revelation. This is why the spiritual awakening is more of a "letting go" of everything you've learned and have been programmed to believe rather than learning something new. Spiritual evolution is about unbecoming the ego persona identity, and rebecoming the true eternal self.

I AM GOD YOU ARE GOD

What would the God inside do? How would the God inside perceive this? What would my human self do? How would my human self perceive this? At any given moment we have the choice to look out from behind our physical eyeballs at the world through the lens of our God self or our human self. The power is in our hands and behind our eyes. When we awaken the divinity within, our hands become Gods hands and our eyes become Gods eyes. That is the goal.

GOD ABOVE IS YOU BELOW

***Holographic Wholeness

If you take a cup of ocean water out of the ocean, the contents of the cup is the same as the ocean, just more concentrated. The contents of the cup being separated from the ocean, doesn't mean you call it something else. It is still the ocean. In the illusion of 3D with separate bodies we seem separated from each other and God, but we are the same. We are all connected through a divine web of etheric light and we are and will always be connected to the Almighty Creator.

You are a spark of the divine, a piece of God, and a piece is part of the whole. If you cut a hologram in half, each half contains whole views of the entire holographic image. The same is true if you cut out a small piece – even a tiny fragment will still contain the whole picture. You are this holographic wholeness of the One Creator Light-God within human form. You do not need healing, you are already healed.

When we look at ourselves in this perspective we realize we are healed in God's eyes and in our God eyes. This is a completely different way to look at ourselves and the world – a shift in perception from 3D to 5D. In 3D we need healing, in 5D we just need remembering. So why don't we call it something else, how about LIFTING? We are already HEALED, WHOLE and PERFECT. AHO.

***Healing on the Bathroom Floor

I have had multiple experiences of instant healing. I shared a profound experience in sunflower one with the wart on my hand. I delivered another one to myself during the time I lived in the White Tara Buddha Ohana. I woke up in the middle of the night feeling sick to my stomach. At first I thought it was the skinny pop I binged on earlier. Then I started shaking and getting really hot with fever. My landlords who lived upstairs both recently had a bad flu, so I worried at first I caught something from them.

I quickly caught that thought as it entered my mind and countered it with, No, I don't get sick. However, I got worse so I crawled out of bed to the bathroom and sat over the toilet in complete nausea. I was scared that it came on so fast and out of the blue.

I started praying to Archangel Raphael, one of my guardian angels for divine healing. Archangel Raphael usually helps me but not that night. I collapsed into the child's pose on the cold floor next to the toilet thinking to myself, I need to bring this up a notch. So I chanted over and over again, "I am God, I don't get sick, I am God, sickness doesn't live in my body, I am God, I am perfect health, light and divinity, I am God, I am God, I am God. I am the light, I am the light, I am the light."

I didn't just chant, I put every ounce of my focus, heart and soul into the affirmations. God is only love, goodness and joy. So if I am God, then germs, viruses, and illness can't live in my physical vessel. Everything is energy and vibration. Germs and illnesses live in the frequency of 100 Hz or so and I live in a higher frequency of God light so they can't touch me.

I fell asleep in child pose, not sure for how long-maybe 20 minutes, and when I woke up I was 100% better. I felt no sickness at all. I got up, went back to bed and woke up in the morning feeling fabulous. This is not a miracle, it's a normal! When you come to really KNOW who you are you can create "A normal" as well. I've had other experiences of instant healing when I shifted my conscious awareness to the truth of who I am. God is only love, joy, goodness, and purity. Can you picture God with the flu?

Take back your power, take back your health.
Be your own doctor.

We have been trained to not believe in ourselves. Others know better than us- our teachers, doctors, parents, psychics, counselors, the news, television, actors, athletes, Dr.Oz, Oprah. When we rely on an outside source for our internal validation, answers and advice we give our power away and this in turn creates our bondage. This is a different kind of slavery- mental and spiritual slavery-but it's still slavery. Don't you think it's strange that we can be walking around with a disease in our body, like cancer, and not even know it?

***The ONE

Looking back it makes sense I called in my Hawaiian Beloved to help me finally heal this last deep wound of finding the true love within. After Fearless Freedom was published I went right back into the mind loops and questioning. I was not walking my talk 100%. I was living from the confusion of my mind and not the clarity of my heart.

Right before *Fearless Freedom* was published I had a psychic reading with one of my clients. I have never had a psychic reading before but I adored my client and she frequently gave me messages from Spirit during our yoga/Qigong sessions that were right on the money. I thought why not?

As well intentioned as this beautiful medium was, she had no idea the monster created from the information she shared with me. She told me I would meet "THE ONE" and he would be my business partner and husband, all rolled up in a perfect package. I would never have to worry about doing it all by myself anymore. He would be my videographer and take care of legal matters. We would meet at one of my book events- definitely by the summer solstice on June 21st. We would know each other instantly by the dance in our hearts. I had that reading recorded on my phone and repeated it in my head daily.

Although eager with anticipation for "The One" to enter my stratosphere, it brought even more anxiety to my already nerve wracking book events. It wasn't bad enough that I had to share my life in public, every single event I was also looking around wondering, "Is he the one? Could it be him? Is he here? Maybe he'll come later…what will I say? Will we recognize each other?" It was a mind trip. By June I still hadn't met "the ONE" but had the idea stuck in the back of my mind that it would happen by the summer solstice. I had one more book event left. I was lost in the mind loops and insane in the membrane.

***June 9th, Strawberry Full Moon Drum Circle

I had made arrangements for an employee from Fios to come to the event to interview me about my book and film the drum circle I had planned as part of the event. The whole thing was to be broadcasted on television. I had spoken with the man from Fios over the phone a couple of times but hadn't met him in person yet.

When we met at the beach for the interview he felt like an old friend I just bumped into again. There was an immediate familiar connection. I felt comfortable around him and wanted to stay by his side; but I tore myself away since I was the main feature of the drum circle.

Could this be him? I couldn't help but question. After all he was a videographer, we had instant familiar connection and ease. It was June 9th and time was almost out. I was taken aback a little, because I didn't know the ONE was going to be in a black wrapper- not that I was complaining.

We became fast friends. He was solid and so supportive of me and my divine purpose.

I approached my brother Sita for guidance because I was so confused. I was trying to fit him into the psychics reading of being the "ONE." She straight out said to me, "It's your ego brother." I agreed with her, "Yes, you're right." I think she was surprised at my response but I was changing, softening. I wanted to evolve and be free no matter what, so I was open to advice. A few years prior and I would have been defensive and angry, protecting my ego at all costs.

The romantic connection…it just wasn't there for me. I tried, I wanted it to be, however you can't force something like that. I tortured myself- but only for a month or so. Thankfully we are still good friends, because he is a man I never want to not have in my life. He was and is truly a blessing.

Shortly after I was invited to a psychic reading event by a friend. I told her "Thank you, but no thank you." She was surprised by the firmness in my voice, "I will not allow any one to put any thoughts in my head. I am the Creator of my Reality and no one else!"

Lesson learned. Even the best psychics are only 50% right, anyway. Free will is our gift from God and it makes predicting the future, especially an exact date nearly impossible. There are various possible timelines and free will choice can cause any number of unpredictable things to happen. On the earth plane, time is linear. In higher dimensions there is no linear time, all is the NOW moment. That's what Einstein meant when he said, "Time is an illusion." Reality is fluid, whichever reality we focus on is the one we will experience.

Destiny and sacred contracts that we make before we incarnate exist, but because of temporary amnesia and/or free will, souls will sometimes make a break or go outside their planned contracts. Every soul has free will and no one, including the angels, higher beings or God herself can interfere with free will.

PETAL 7

Kismet Connections

***The Whale

My new dear friend came bearing a gift, a unique gift, that I will treasure for the rest of my life. A few days after the drum circle event I asked him if we could redo the interview. I was reverting back to the insecure girl only focused on my flaws. I decided I didn't like what I had said in the interview, what I was wearing, that I was squinting my face from the sun in my eyes, blah, blah, blah. My new friend was definitely trained very well, he replied without hesitation, "Sure."

The day we were scheduled to re-interview I received a text from him in the morning...."Good morning, I was revisiting your interview and first of all, I don't know why you want to redo it, you were fantastic, second of all there were whales in the ocean behind you." He had my complete attention. I assumed he's just saying that because he didn't want to put in the time and effort to do it over so I called him. "What do you mean there were whales in the ocean?"

He replied that he was looking more carefully at the interview and he noticed something in the background come out of the ocean behind me. He zoomed in and played it over and over to make sure what he was seeing was correct and even got a second opinion. It was a whale that jumped out of the ocean the exact moment I was talking about how scared and panicked I was the day my memoir was published and I realized that the whole world would know my story.

I was speechless. (Doesn't happen to often)

"Hello, hello," he says, "Are you there? Soulfire hello? She must have hung up," and he hangs up the phone.

Standing in the kitchen holding the phone in my hand with tears welling up in my eyes in disbelief, I call him back. "Use the interview, I don't care what I said, what I look like, what I was wearing...there were whales!" I exclaimed.

"Okaaaay," he responds, not understanding my jubilation.

It was one of those moments when you experience something that is so profound for you, yet if you know the minute you try to explain it to someone with words, the words could never do the feeling justice.

I try to explain to him anyway, "You don't understand what this means to me. My father passed away during the dark time I was going through two years ago when my Beloved walked out on me. I was in such despair and heartache that as soon as I found out my Dad transitioned, I prayed to him, "Dad, you were never there for me when you were alive, could you be there for me now. I need you. Please help me, help my heart, I am broken." I took a deep breath, and instantly I felt the heavy sadness leave my heart. It was miraculous.

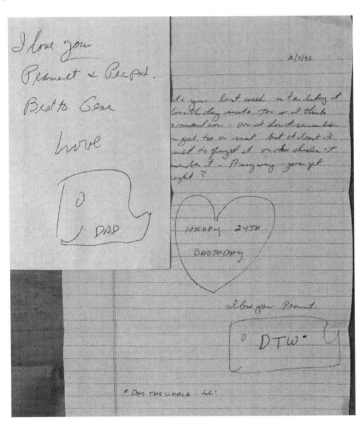

Ever since that moment I call on my Dad all the time and I feel him in my life. He was disabled in his body when he was alive, but when he transitioned and left his body, his spirit was able to be with me. I continued, "My Dad called himself the Whale."

Whale was also the name of our boat, and how he signed his notes and letters, Dad the Whale with a hand drawn picture of a whale.

Are we just a tiny speck in the multiverse? If the universe can orchestrate that perfect moment with perfect timing for me specifically, what are the chances that the universe pretty much knows what's going on with all beings all the time? It reminds me that even when we are feeling small and insignificant, the loving benevolent universe has got an eye on us, and we are not alone. We have more support than we can possibly fathom. We matter.

***Dad in Hawaii

Energy never dies, it just changes form.
Since souls don't have a form they can get around a lot easier. It seems my Dad followed me to Hawaii. He has appeared numerous times in my life when I spoke to him. The first time was Thanksgiving 2018. I had been in Hawaii for less than two months and as much as I loved Hawaii, I was still lost and trying to find my place in the sun.

That morning my friend picked me up and we went to the pier to find the dolphins. A dream on my bucket list was to swim with the dolphins naturally in the wild. As we drove closer we could see a bunch of boats gathered, a good sign that there were dolphins.

We hurried and parked, walked to the pier and had to swim about a mile out to reach where the dolphins were gathered. My friend was an ironman and in great shape. While I too am in great shape I wasn't in the same category. So as we were swimming he gained a large distance on me and I just let him go. There's no way I could keep up with him. Next thing I know one of the boats started playing a song, very loudly, or at least this is how I heard: I Can't Help Falling In Love With You, originally by Elvis but this song was done by a Hawaiian artist. I stopped swimming and treaded water in disbelief. I was by myself, the boats and other swimmers were all ahead of me by a couple hundred feet.

I started crying, tears welling up in my goggles. How is this happening? This was my father's song. He played it every night belting it out in the living room-probably drunk... but, oh well. It brought me back to my childhood hearing him sing it.

My friend turned back to look for me and I just waved him on. I was overwhelmed with emotion. I couldn't swim, my breathing was much too heavy and I was too emotional.

Just then I looked down in the ocean and there they were! A pod of dolphins swimming around so close to me that I could reach out and touch them. My heart was overjoyed. I couldn't believe the dolphins had come right to me. I got the opportunity to have them all to myself for the next ten minutes. I laughed with glee, cried tears of joy and thanked them for showing up for me. It was a Thanksgiving I'll never forget.

The dolphins have come to me numerous times since my initiation into my new family. They come to remind me to play, have fun and be in my highest joy. Don't take life so seriously, they telepathically say to me. I need this remembrance from them as I can be very intense and focused at times. I remind myself to keep the balance.

***More Magical Moments

Another serendipitous event happened when I was driving up the coast taking Karma for an adventure up north. I had just gotten Gracie running steadily and felt I needed to get out of town. It had been a while since I thought of my Dad so I started talking to him. Then I turned on the radio and a song came on that I hadn't heard in fifteen years. It was a song I would sing to the people in my life that crossed over. I got the God bumps all over my body tenfold. I felt like my whole body was about to take off into space, the energy was pouring through me, I wasn't sure what was happening.

I then said out loud, "I haven't seen whales in a while so if this is you Dad I want to see a whale jump out of the ocean." I looked to my left into the vast Pacific and just as I did a whale jumped out of the ocean. I couldn't believe it. Then it jumped again and again. I pulled over as soon as I could find a safe space along the highway. I was so happy, giggling like a little girl. I found a tree to sit under with Karma to soak in the magic of the moment and the enveloping love I felt.

"A magical presence is created when one truly lives in harmony
with all living things." ~Grace Mantle

***What tribe do I come from?

I was invited to attend the Sacred Native Sundance Ceremony in 2018 in Alberta Canada with First Nation Cree. This was a dream come true for me. I went with Dr. Bruce Lipton who is one of my favorite scientists and authors. I love his teachings, his sense of humor, and the way he communicates makes quantum physics understandable which is an almost impossible task!

To be respectful of their tradition I won't go into detail except when it pertains to my direct experience. In one of the ceremonies called the 'shaking tent' we each got the opportunity to ask the grandfathers a question. There were probably at least 50 of us sitting in the tent. I went first as my native friend nudged me, "Ask your question, ask your question." I asked the question, "What tribe do I come from?"

A couple of years prior my (native) grandmother came through in a spiritual channel to give me a birthday present. She knew I was always curious about my heritage. I had learned I am part Native American and had lifetimes as a medicine woman. My daughter and my grandmother were as well. I was told I was from the First Nation but I didn't know what that meant. When I met Grandmother Cher from Sundance, she hugged me and told me I was native for sure because I had a little bear next to me nuzzling my leg.

So when I was sitting in the dark tent with the sacred energy of the grandfathers every hair on my body was at attention. I was hanging on to their answer with so much of my heart.

The answer was not brief, in fact it was quite lengthy, probably the longest answer out of all the questions. In the end they never told me specifically what I wanted to hear. Of course, I realized the wisdom of not knowing.

They said, "We all come from the ashes, we all come from the same blood." That was the short of the long.

I got it. Even though it's not what I wanted to hear, I received their message loud and clear. It doesn't matter which tribe you are from. What matters is that our very essence is the same. We are the same, one blood, one spirit, one family, one LOVE...in many different forms. To think we're alone and separate is an illusion. The warrior spirit of our ancestors lives In the earth, in the trees, in the rocks, In the water, in your blood and in the air we breathe. Soldier on.

Being adopted and not knowing half of my nationality played with my self esteem and self worth my entire life until I woke up and realized that it doesn't matter. And in fact not knowing makes it easier to connect with everyone of all colors, races, tribes, and nationalities. In the back of my mind I have the thought, I could be one of them. The highest truth is that I am them and they are me. I'm now grateful for not knowing.

I will never take a DNA test. I have one, it was gifted to me for my birthday a few years ago, but after I reflected on it, I realized it's not necessary. In my opinion, it's another way to perpetuate our limited perspective that keeps us in a box separate and divided. Most old souls have been everything already anyway, we have been male, female, black, white, mother, father, hero, villain, etc. The truth is it really doesn't matter because WE are ONE.

I am because you are.

***Sparrow Hawk

During another ceremony I received my native name: Sparrow Hawk. I was confused at first- I thought I was given two names, but realized Sparrow Hawk is a type of hawk. I have a deep connection to the hawk- it's my animal power spirit.

One memorable hawk story happened to me in upstate New York. I had just dropped off my daughter at a farm and was on my way home back to Long Island. I hadn't realized that using the GPS drained my cell phone battery and my cheap phone car charger had stopped working. I couldn't tell which way was north, south, east or west because I was deep in the hills and the sun had started setting.

I got anxious. I do not like driving in the dark, especially somewhere I have never been that had steep hills, twists and turns. I was a couple of hours away from home and wasn't even sure which way was the way back to my daughter.

I relaxed, took a deep breath and called upon Hawk to guide me. I thought from my heart, "I know you can hear me and I know you can see me from way up there, please help me get home." I didn't know what else to do. All of a sudden I heard, "beep." I looked at my cell phone and it started charging. It gave me enough juice to get home safely. Thank you Hawk.

Hawk is **Io** in Hawaiian and another one of my Amakua's. Every time I was broken down in my car, which was often at the start, the Io was circling above. It made me feel safe and connected. I learned this majestic bird is found only on the Big Island. Do you think this is a coincidence that I ended up here? I think not. Hawk spirit is watching over me.

***Fierce

When I told the chief my name, he was silent for a minute. Then he looked me directly in the eyes and said with intensity, "When the sparrow hawk swoops down to catch its prey, it grabs it with its talons so strongly and never lets go," as he imitated the bird with his arm and hand.

That was it. That was all he said. I meditated on it and realized I am like the sparrow hawk. I have the same focus, intensity, strength, swiftness and loyalty and I will never give up. I will never stop fighting for you, for humanity. I will be your greatest supporter cheering you on, because I believe in you. The sparrow hawk is the embodiment of a fierce warrior in a small package, like my dog Karma (and I). She embodies whole hearted belief and is a fearless Warrior goddess.

The Sparrow Hawk's medicine is: focus, timing, patience Her magic: visionary and ability to see though secret realms. She is symbolic of: **As we practice so shall we become.**

These cosmic connections are like Crack for my soul. They show me
the divine intelligence and sacred interconnectedness of All and remind
me that we are never alone. The image below is not photoshopped, it's
from a cave that is known for showing your aura or the face of your soul
peering back at you. I went hoping to capture my soul on camera, but a
rainbow unicorn appeared. I guess that is my true reflection!

PS. I had the honor of meeting the whale that is at the front of this petal. I got to swim with him and three others in his posse. They were amazing. I felt like they were my guardians. They are Blainville Beaked Whales and are very rare to see and swim with since they are skittish. I floated in the water and they came to me and stayed with me for ten minutes. We shared eye contact and eye threads of the Akash. It was one of the most magical moments I have ever had.

PETAL 8

As Above So Below

THE QUESTION: Is it possible that there's something about life that I don't fully understand and the understanding of which would change everything?

We've been living under a false identity with false beliefs. We've all been living in the "Great Deception." But now the tides have turned, and we are living in the "Great Awakening." Nothing, nothing can stop the sun from shining and the love from loving.

***La: Sun in Hawaiian

The sun is 92 million miles away from the earth but you can still feel it's heat – that's pretty amazing. Even though clouds and storms occupy the sky at times, the sun is still there. No matter who you are, the sun does not discriminate or judge. The sun shines equally on all of us. It shines and gives us life. God is like the sun.

Have you ever squinted your eyes and looked at the sun? You will discover there's a golden ray of the sun's light that beams into your heart center. And no matter where you walk, that golden cord stays with you connected to your heart center. Try it next time you are sun gazing.

We have a metaphysical golden umbilical cord that is attached from our heart womb that goes right to God, the Supreme Creator. If we didn't we wouldn't be here. This golden cord of luminosity is your 'umbilical cord' that connects the unfiltered, pure, unadulterated You of your higher self to the sacred you in human form. No matter how hard you try to deny God, you can't not be God. You may be in your body staying asleep to this fact, but it doesn't change the Truth.

***Having a Human Moment

Isn't it strange that we have to work so hard at being who we are? But I guess that's the point of polarity and duality. For when you wake up and reclaim your divine heritage you will never forget it and never let it go. It will be your most valuable asset.

With God as the main event you begin to have human moments instead of divine moments. It's a flip in consciousness- meaning most of your day you will be living from your higher God consciousness, but sometimes you will forget and slip back into the human conditioning. Those human moments are just temporary amnesia. You can get right back to your winged self by just being aware and rerouting your thoughts back to up high.

It's all practice.

***The God Dream

I had a dream that I was in a classroom and the teacher, who is my brother/spiritual guide Sita, asked the question: "What is the meaning of life?"

One student replied, "To be God."

I raised my hand and answered, "To be God in 3D."

While the first student's answer was true, I simply emphasized the importance of recognizing we will still be here in the polarity of the collective 3D drama of forgetting, fear, pain and separation. It is easy to know you are God when you exist in the higher dimensions and everyone around you knows they are God too. It is not as easy to be God when you are asleep in 3D with the collective. You slip in and out of the dream, the Maya (illusion), the Matrix and the ego mind. Maintaining this high level of awareness is the work when you have woken up.

Having a daily spiritual or energetic practice is crucial, it is a must to keep us in our high VF. It also helps to have a spiritual community of people for support. It can be lonely as you ascend and begin to speak an entirely different language than other people. Other people may think you're "out there," but ironically you're in there!

LIKE ATTRACTS LIKE 100% OF THE TIME

Everything is energy. You are manifesting your perceived reality, whether you are conscious of the process or not. Your VF (vibrational frequency) creates your ER (external reality).. Most of humanity is not conscious therefore creating by default. And their default operating systems are based on false beliefs, that is why we are in the mess we are in.

I know so many spiritual seekers that are stuck and it's from the simple fact that they believe in the above statement except when their life is not going the way they want it, then it's everyone else's fault, certainly not theirs. They are in victim mode.

I recently had a conversation with a spiritually 'awake' friend who was struggling with some life stuff and called me to talk. I made a statement to her which she immediately disregarded saying, "I've done that already." Those words sounded familiar because that is what I used to say when my ego was in charge. She was in denial. She didn't understand that doing a healing once is not over. It is layers and layers of unthreading deep seeded wounds. I stopped offering guidance at that point. She wasn't really asking for advice, she was looking for someone to dump her problems out on, and I'm done being a dumpster! You can't help those who aren't willing to help themselves.

Nothing is happening outside of you, really. Everything that is happening or appearing to you on the outside is a reflection of your thoughts, feelings and beliefs on the inside. It begins within, and until we take full responsibility for that fact we will remain stuck.

The universe responds to our frequency/vibration/resonance. I learned that by looking externally for validation, even from God, my angels and spirit guides, it was still keeping me from my being my own beloved. The validation must come from our own inner being, from our knowing heart and pure true resonance. That is the only way. There is NO thing and NO one that can give you that. Not even God. Because you are God and you must rise to become the God you already are. That is our whole purpose here. We are Gods in progress.

***Christ Consciousness

Then manifestation becomes a thing of the past because true manifestation is not done with willful intent from the power of the mind. That is not the Christed way. The Christed Way is becoming the Christ within. When you embody the Christ Consciousness-the Heart of Christ, living in the knowing of your true divine essence and pure holy resonance, there is nothing to manifest. You have risen to the higher dimensions/realities and the word manifest no longer exists. Manifestation is an energy of the old paradigm. It is a human act of doing in 3D. It's because of the elongation of time, ie., linear time that the word manifestation exists. In 5D we are God BEing. The moment we think about a thing it appears. There is no more manifestation. This is how the loaves of bread and fish instantly appeared for Jesus. He was the master of quantum physics and knew the higher laws of the universe. He embodied his God self one hundred percent.

I'm starting to experience that here in Hawaii with cowrie shells that I'm obsessed with. My favorite necklace, made up of Cowrie shells that I had for over twenty years, fell off one day while swimming in the ocean when I first moved here. Ever since then I have been collecting Cowrie shells to make a new necklace. The ones I collect have to be whole which are not as easy to find as the broken ones. Now I find them everywhere. I can just think about one look down in the sand and it's sitting right there. Instant materialization.

> "Man's chief delusion is his conviction that there are causes other than his own state of consciousness." ~Neville Goddard

***Self Contained Island

We live in a loving benevolent universe, where there is no judgment in the higher realms, no judgment from our Mother Father God/Goddess, the only judgment comes from humans. There is no one, except ourselves, that we have to please or answer to. If your God parents aren't judging you, why allow your human parents to bring their opinions and judgments on to you. Some people spend their entire life trying to please their parents. Our human parents are just as flawed as everybody else walking the earth under the material spell.

The collective is walking around like zombies, "Must get things, must get things, must be perfect, must be perfect, must have everyone like and accept me, must have everyone like and accept me, but most importantly must buy lots of things."

To become a master we must have mastery within, mastery of ourselves first. We must relearn how to be self contained without adoration, accolades, acknowledgment or validation from anyone or anything. I learned this in my unfolding. There were times when I was being authentic and true to myself and then there were times when I was being what I thought everyone else wanted me to be and wanted to hear. I was playing both sides of the coin, so to say. We must become a self balancing island, a self balancing master, free from the constraints and constructs of a spiritually void society that doesn't have to know anything more than God is within, God is you.

We have the divine link to God that validates our every breath.

The ability to contain self worth automatically no matter what is hard for some of the old souls who have had lifetimes after lifetimes in subservience and come into this lifetime with no self worth or so limited they have to have external validation, which was me. I used to ponder how some people were so confident and sure of themselves. It was fascinating to me. I'd look at them like they were ET's wondering how they got that way. It's a trait I admire so much.

That is why the task at hand is to know thyself. Know thyself as a piece of God, self contained, self balancing, one who is able to channel truth for oneself and is the link to our higher self. We can be a collector of information but don't let it validate you. You don't need validation. You are valid because you are.

"Whatever doubt may rise, it cannot rise without the rising of you-the first to have risen-who raised it. Therefore the primal doubt, namely that of not knowing who you are, is the root of all doubts." ~A

***Questions, Questions, Questions

I have lived many many many incarnations on this earth with an inquisitive mind. I have always been a questioner. The same holds true for this lifetime. I am a seeker of light, like my brother, but the difference is he/she has the inner knowing and I have always been a questioner. My brother used to say to me, "Can you just come to know? You are the wonderer of understanding, brother, can you just come to know?" This has been a large part of my unfolding. I don't know if I'll ever stop asking questions, that is the nature of my mind. But as I start to shift into 'being' more and living in VF and true resonance with my heart versus mind loops, the questions cease.

In the beginning of your awakening it's crucial to question everything. Discernment is critical. Hopefully though there comes a point in your spiritual evolution when you just come to know and are content with all that is happening around you as the observer sitting in a space of neutrality and presence. This is my practice now.

"In the language of duality alone are questions and answers. In non-duality they are not." ~A

***Loving Your True Self

You can say you love yourself, but saying it and being it are two different things. I used to say I loved myself all the time but I didn't know what being your own beloved actually was until I went through the catalytic relationship with HB. I was loving my form, not my true self. Loving yourself means being in alignment with the highest resonance of your spiritual heart, being authentically you.

Years ago a sister asked me at a drum circle, "How do you love yourself?" It was the perfect question to which I had no answer. At least not in words. I took her into the middle of the drum circle and started dancing with her, twirling her around smiling and being in our highest joy. I had no idea how much work I had ahead of me in the next few years. I thought I was loving myself but I was not quite there yet.

***Delia

Another drum circle I attended in Long Island showed me the power in loving yourself. I couldn't help but notice this little girl who was having what looked like the time of her life. She was in her happy place dancing unabashedly free in her little dress. She didn't care or notice anything or anyone around her. She was in the moment, pure happiness and presence. She was being her God self. Almost everyone was watching her with smiles on their faces. She was just a pure delight to observe.

Children are special souls. They know. They, like we were once, are born with the connection to their God self and to God, intact and strong. They still carry magic in their heart. They know how to be their own beloved because they have not forgotten yet.

There was another person dancing like the little girl, an older woman, maybe in her sixties, dressed like a cute hippie. She also looked like she was having the time of her life dancing in pure joy. I noticed the people sitting in the circle observing her but their reactions were not smiles, they were sneers, laughter, and judgment. To be honest that really bummed me out and hurt my heart. Luckily this woman did not notice, or maybe she did notice but did not care. When we see a four year old wearing her princess dress in the supermarket we smile and say how cute. When we see a fifty year old wearing her princess dress into the supermarket we are wondering if it's Halloween or she forgot to take her meds. Being in our innocence and pure heart is the secret to a joyful life but society has already labeled and proclaimed us crazy if we express it in any way that is not socially acceptable in our ego boxed in world.

I say wear your fucking princess dress, fairy wings and rainbow unicorn hat if it's authentically calling you. I do. And I don't care.

That's when you walk from place to place and nothing can touch you, no jeers, no judgment, no angry words, no situation, you become a more stable, more balanced human, walking empowered in the knowing of who you are with magic and joy in your heart.

I DON'T CARE

It's empowering to not care about what other people think about you. Say it out loud...I don't care, I don't care, I don't care. Stand in the light of your truth, stand in the light of your strength, your creativity, uniqueness and your divinity. Don't let anyone make you feel less than or diminish your light. Let them go, forget about them, without bitterness, without resentment, just go... Buh-bye.

For those of you who read my first sunflower you might recall I was married once very briefly. In that relationship my husband forbade me to curse. I couldn't even say "hell" without him scolding me. I accommodated his request because I was lost and trying to please him. Gag me with a spoon! Why do I curse a lot in my writing? Because I fucking can. And it's fucking liberating.

**Shush me no more.
I don't care.**

It's all God anyway.

AHO AHO AHO AHO AHO AHO AHO AHO AHO

***This... WE UNDERSTAND IT BUT WE DON'T PRACTICE IT

If we spend all our time focused on our bodies, the external, and living in our minds we will never come to the place of heart centered rooted security and becoming our own beloved. We must stop the insanity and change our habits and routine. If you want change in your life you must change your life.

There has to be a reason compelling enough for you to change. That is why crisis serves a purpose. However, there does not need to be a crisis for change to be born. How about reasons like: you will feel better, you will look better, you'll stop aging, you will smile, laugh, be in joy and oh yea, you'll get everything you want! Is that reason enough?

Self-Sabotage-Let's Talk About It
***Da nile

The greatest obstacle to healing is denial that anything is imbalanced in the first place. I know many prideful people that will never admit that they need help or healing. They are too preoccupied with keeping their ego intact, which is self preservation of the wrong self. It's a way the ego keeps you in stagnation and suffering. I understand living in denial from the ego mind. I did it most of my life, until I valued my freedom over everything. We need to find freedom from the ego, not for the ego.

If you are alive today and over 25 years old chances are you're in need of healing-you are the walking wounded like everyone else. There's no shame in admitting it. Actually, admitting it can be very freeing. For many many years I was in denial of my need for healing. When I was accused of having anger issues from my partner, I'd scream, "Eff you! No I don't," stomp away and slam the door. When I finally accepted myself, all of me, my anger, rage, pride, anxiety, unstable mind, sadness and grief, it opened up the space for healing.

***Stuck in your False Paradigm

Another common obstacle is that many people cannot handle changing or looking differently at the mental constructs of what the world has taught them about who they are. Their intellect is too strong and their ego mind has taken over. They live in their head, reading the 'headlines' all day. People are too afraid to change their beliefs and as a result they hold on with everything to keep their beliefs intact even if the beliefs don't serve their highest good. When you are in fear consciousness, where the collective vibrates at, the amygdala part of the brain actually shuts down. Fear causes the mind to be closed to new thoughts, ideas and beliefs.

***Really?

One of my closest and dearest friends who is no longer in my life said to me sarcastically shortly after my memoir Fearless Freedom was published, "Not everyone can be Soulfire." That stung because of how she said it, but mostly because she missed the whole fucking point of my life. I didn't come here to suffer for nothing lady!

I came into this incarnation to experience the depths of despair and heartache in every chapter of my life for you. I chose it to help humanity awaken and rise into their true divine essence by going to the suffering of the earth to understand then transmute the darkness to light for others to heal.

I am the poster child for, "If I can do it, you can too!"

Anyway, why would you want to be me? You are you and I am me. You are here for a reason. Your journey with all your lessons, growth, ups and downs is just as beautiful and meaningful as anyones. No soul is greater than another, that is just silly ego talk and thinking. WE are ONE. If we are one, how can one soul matter more?

I am no greater than you. I am you in a higher dimension. I have the same struggles, insecurities, challenges, maybe more than you or maybe not. They might just show up in different disguises. Maybe the only difference right now is that I remember- I'm a step ahead to pave the way and create new energetic pathways for you to follow.

***I don't have time, blah, blah, blah

A third obstacle is the excuse, "I don't have time." This is the human ego mind keeping you stuck in your everyday routines so that you will never find the power and peace within. We all have the same amount of time in a day, what you do with it and how you prioritize it is a different story. When you invest in yourself the dividends you receive will be one hundred fold. If you look at the priorities in your life differently you will make time for yourself and your healing.

Let's take it high: Let's go quantum: The only time that exists in the universe is now. The only space that exists in the universe is here. Now and here is the only reality.

If you attempt to exist in this non times or non realities of past and future you will become fragmented and lose vital life force. The correct spiritual practice to master time/space is to bring all your consciousness awareness in the now/here-becoming present which is presence. This is where the magic of life occurs. When you become present your consciousness levels are greatly elevated and linear time as we know it expands for you and allows you to get what you need accomplished.

Four Steps

I'VE OUTLINED FOUR STEPS I use to process trauma and perceived imbalances so I could transform spiritually, raise my vibration and KNOW that I am my own BEloved.

1. **REVEAL**
2. **FEEL**
3. **HEAL**
4. **RISE**

REVEAL REVEAL REVEAL

"People will do anything, no matter how absurd, to
avoid facing their own souls."
~CG Jung

***Have a Holy Conversation

Sacred solitude is necessary for step one. If you never spend any time with yourself how will you get to know your Self? You're probably thinking that's a silly question, of course you know yourself, I am myself. You are you after all.

The Self I'm referring to is your divine self- the non physical part of you that is mostly who you are. We are multidimensional beings and part of us exists in 3D linear time and space reality of earth. This is our human self. But the majority of our being is up in higher dimensions having a grand ole time. Don't you want to hang with that part of you?

I never had a best friend as an adult, but received one during one of the hardest darkest times in my life. She was an angel. I looked up to her, she was incredible. She used to tell everyone I was her best friend and that made me feel so good inside. However, she got so busy working, dancing and socializing I said to her bravely one day, "What's the point in having a best friend if we never spend any time together?" She received my message gracefully and agreed with me. After that she made it a point to spend quality time with me.

The same holds true for ourselves. If we want to develop and nurture a strong solid relationship with our deep inner Self we need to spend quality time with our Self. Spending time in quiet sacred solitude is the perfect time to review, reflect and recalibrate, or simply be. This is a great time to talk to your Self. There is a societal belief that people who talk to themselves are cray-crays. Well, I'm officially nuts then because there are days when the only person I talk to is my Self. There's Truth to: Me, Myself and I.

Have a holy conversation with yourself or just ask yourself the questions, "Hey higher Self, how are you doing today?" Or "Is there anything I need to know that would help me on my path?" And then quiet your thoughts and see what comes through. You might hear nothing at first, then later in the day a message might filter down when you're least expecting it. In the alpha state of brain waves- present moment meditation- divine guidance has an easier chance of trickling in. Sometimes trying too hard to hear or receive a message actually blocks it from coming.

Overfilling the to-do list and calendar leaving no time to be alone can cause physical and energetic drain. It's an avoidance trick of the shadow who fears change and the unknown. If you want to evolve into your God self and ascend into 5D you must carve out sacred solitude to do the work. It is in times of sacred solitude that balance is regained.

Being alone allows us the opportunity to review, reflect and confront our actions and examine the inner-self. Most importantly we can dive deeply into our Self and rediscover the love within. This part of the process requires self-honesty and self-awareness. Ask yourself the question, what patterns keep repeating in my life or my relationships that keep me stuck, closed and not in my highest joy? Then listen for the answer.

***My Spiritual Grandfather

I learned this next gem from Kryon. If you are not familiar with him, he is a Light Being who loves and supports humanity and has been delivering messages through Lee Carroll since 1989. Kryon has never taken a human body. He is pure God love and wisdom. He's like my spiritual grandfather. I love his messages.

I followed Kryon's guidance for myself and it took my relationship with my Self to a whole new level. Kryon's offering for making first contact with your God self:

Sitting quietly alone in your sacred space or with your sacred altar, acknowledge your divinity in whatever way is authentic for you. It could be as simple as "Hey, God within, how's it going? I don't think we were ever formally introduced. I am_____ ...which obviously you know. Duh. You are my divine compass and way home. Let's do this!"

The point is that it doesn't have to be all formal. It has to come from you in your language and verbiage. I'm constantly having silly conversations with my God self, laughing out loud at some of the things I say and I know for sure they are laughing with me. They (I) know how quirky I am.

Then you make the love connection. It's especially important to be authentic or it will not work. Tell yourself, your divine higher self that you are sorry you have been unconsciously ignoring them for your whole life but now you are ready to work in tandem. Then from your heart tell your higher self that you love them. Simply say, "I love you." with sincerity.

You will know you've made that connection when you feel the God bumps or tingling all over your body. That is confirmation. If it's not authentic and you're not saying it with genuine feeling behind the words, it will not work. When I went through this exercise, I cried, big surprise there! It was so affirming to my soul, it made me feel so much more secure and solid within, yet so light and free. It was like a piece of myself was returned. Once you've made it, there is no going back. You're homies for life and eternity.

***Erroneous Beliefs Revealed

You might uncover during the reveal stage that you've adopted someone else's beliefs or are holding on to an old belief that no longer holds validity for you.

I had two beliefs running in the background that kept me from finding the beloved within:

1. What if I never find someone that loves me as much as he does?
2. Good men are hard to find, especially here on this island.

The first one was from my own mind and the second one was from someone else's. Either way, I took them in and made them my reality. These misguided beliefs are based in fear and lack, and while I wanted to be with my Beloved, the erroneous beliefs running in the background allowed disharmony to creep in.

The first belief was replaced with a better belief: "The only person that will love me as much as anyone else loves me is ME." And that's the understanding I had to come to on my own.

The second belief I took in out of fear. I'm surrounded by good men, they are NOT hard to find. I have so many good male friends and soul brothers in my life because that IS my true belief. I am so grateful to the good men in my life. If you are one of them reading this, thank you. I love you.

Just because someone said something doesn't make it true.

***What is Truth?

All that a truth is is something that somebody else focused upon, that's what made it a truth. When a whole lot of people focus on something it becomes true in enough of their experience then you say this is a reality (or consensus reality.) It is only true because somebody focused upon it. It doesn't have to be your truth, that's not logical. Reality is a strong word. A better description is perceived reality which is based on our perceptions. As our perceptions change within, our perceived realities change with out.

We are conditioned to focus on the negative. I see this truth that I do not want, but I will focus on it. How does that make sense? We need to be divine filters and make sure we are not haphazardly taking in beliefs that do not resonate with what we know deep down is our truth.

What is your truth?...

FEEL FEEL FEEL

***Pain is Perception

Pain can be a powerful teacher but nobody wants to be its student. Feeling into the pain allows us to heal and then free the stagnant energy, otherwise it will remain stuck in our tissues, cells, our physical body, and in a vortex around our auric field when not addressed. This is the stage that I avoided my entire life until I had no other choice.

Turn the mirror toward you and honestly face yourself- peer deeply into the depths of your soul. Face and feel the pain and release it to be transmuted back to the light. There are many different tools given to humanity at this time to go through this process. It is not a one stop shop.

I was in such a habit of living from my mind that I temporarily stopped feeling. I was numb. I thought I could process my emotions through my mind and that would be enough to heal. That was incorrect. We must feel through our heart. Healing with the mind does not work.

Sometimes you have to break down before you can break
through.

Sometimes being in the fetal position on the ground is when true heal-ing can take place. There is a grace to falling to your knees in complete heartbreak and surrender. The hardness softens, the walls around your heart crumble and the light shines through.

"The wound is the place where the Light enters you." ~ Rumi

In times of the greatest despair is when you are most surrounded by the holy spirit, your angels, and your guides to comfort you. Know that you are not broken, nothing is wrong with you, you are not defective, you are human and you are healing.

Let the true feelings surface, don't push them back down. Feel them, no mat-ter how icky or horrible they feel. They aren't you, they are an imbalanced unresolved energy that you have been holding on to, but it's time to free this energy and transmute it back to the light. This is your path to liberation.

Remember...

> **It is because you loved yourself so deeply, you said yes to the current challenges of your life.**
> **It is because you loved yourself so deeply, you said yes to the current challenges of your life.**
> **It is because you loved yourself so deeply, you said yes to the current challenges of your life.**

> **YOU ARE NOT A VICTIM. Let that one sink in.**

***You are the Chooser of it All!

You chose your experiences, all of them, even your parents. What!? When I first heard this statement I knew it to be true. I felt it as sure as the sky is blue but then something in my life would go awry and I would scream to the universe, "There's no way I would create this for me. WTF.

This sucks. I'm tired of this shit. I'm done universe!" I don't know how many times I yelled, "I'm done!" to the universe. It's laughable because we are never done.

When you are in full blown suffering, hearing, "you chose this" is not what you want to hear, but it's the truth. Free will choice is our gift from the Creator when we come down to the blue planet. You might not remember you chose it, but that doesn't mean you didn't choose it.

Once you've learned the reason you created the event you can look back and see the wisdom and reason for the struggle and dark nights of the soul. Knowing your own darkness helps you to know the darkness of others. It brings more empathy and compassion. It also returns the fractured parts of you back to your wholeness once again.

> "Until you make the unconscious conscious, it will direct your
> life and you will call it fate." ~CG Jung

An acronym I find helpful for this processing: **FEAR**

FACE
EVERYTHING
AND
RISE

Old souls usually choose the more challenging life lessons. This is mainly that the greater the challenges to overcome, the wiser the soul. For it is indeed under severe pressure that the rarest diamonds are formed

***God Knows Your Heart
When the burden you created for yourself becomes too much I find this valuable prayer really helps. Sit quietly in your own space, go within your inner sanctuary and talk to God. God knows your heart.

"I release these feelings of bondage I hold so tightly around my
heart to you God. Please take my burdens and transmute them
back to pure divine light and send it out to bless others with it.
Thank you. Amen."

This action of releasing it not only lifts you from the limitations and burdens it holds, but also all the energy you are holding can be transmuted
and released where it is most needed. Each time you give anything over
you do a great service to yourself and the world. This certainly reframes
our suffering.

A part of what is no longer serving you has returned back to God, back
to the light and your Wings are ready to take new flight. How beautiful
is this.

***Not a Final Destination

After we go through the feeling stage which can take one session or
days, weeks, years, it depends…everyone's journey is different and we
all created different burdens for ourselves, we can integrate the energy
and truly heal. Honor your feelings and honor yourself in this stage,
but make sure you don't get stuck at this stage- in the feelings of despair, sadness, and grief. This is only a temporary stop or layover, not
a final destination. I know many spiritual seekers that are always "in
process."

Remember WE DIDN'T COME HERE TO SUFFER, and wallow in the
darkness. We chose to experience polarity to learn from it and find the
joy. We didn't come forth into physical existence because we needed to.
We came to earth because we WANTED to. There's a big difference. It
was our choosing. And we certainly didn't come here to suffer then die.
Who would choose that?

Be open to receiving healing in all different ways from different sources.

***Sticks and Stones May Break My Bones and Names Hurt Me

Before I moved to Hawaii during one of my last walks with Karma through my neighborhood in Long Island I encountered a group of young boys. They rode their bikes by me laughing and jeering at my eyes. Really? I thought to myself. This is still happening!? I am forty nine years old and I'm still being made fun of because of my eyes.

It brought me back to the time I was driving home along the parkway when the girl in the car next to me out of the blue started making fun of my eyes, laughing and jeering at me from her car, then plummeted her soft drink at my windshield.

When I was a young girl it was brutal. Brookhaven Day Camp was Brookhaven Torture Camp for me. Everyday I hid from this awful boy who tirelessly chanted jap, jap, jap at me. In high school I was made fun of and my brother relentlessly teased me until I ran to my room crying in shame.

This is my trigger word. It gets me to the core of my wound. and it hurts. And no matter how much work I do on myself, how much I evolve in my consciousness if someone calls me 'Chink,' I still feel the sting in my heart.

Looking different and standing out was no longer an issue in Hawaii. No more getting picked on and made fun of. Here my sensitive soul was safe and the night of January 13, 2019 delivered the best healing balm for this deep wound I'd carried for most of my life. I will be forever thankful to the Aina, to Hawaii, for delivering this healing energy to me. I will forever celebrate it as a Healing Day. (Coincidence this is my HB birthday?)

I watched the movie, Mao's Last Dancer- a true story about a Chinese man, Li, who left his family and Communist China and came to America to follow his dreams and dance ballet. Li speaks very little English, except for what he learns from his pocket Chinese/English dictionary. One day he asks innocently of the man who he's staying with the meaning of a word since he could not find it in his pocket dictionary.

Li asked, "What does Chink mean?" I felt my gut do a flip. This scene had my full attention. A look of hurt momentarily swept across Ben's face, then he responded with such an insightful and grace filled reply,

"Well you know when the curtains on stage are slightly open and the light comes through? That is called a chink. They are calling you chink because they are seeing the light in you."

After hearing these words I cried so much. It felt like I was crying for every single time someone mocked me with that word. Tears can be transformational.

The kicker is, I tried watching two other movies before I watched Mao's Last Dancer, but my computer refused to play them. Healing comes through all sorts of channels when the Universe gives you a gift. A word that had caused me so much agony throughout my life was transformed and now it carries a new meaning and vibration.

***A Long Time Healing Happened

While writing this sunflower some old deep memories resurfaced. My best friend from college popped into my mind. I hadn't thought about her in years, as a matter of fact I hadn't spoken to her in nearly thirty years! She could not forgive me for what I did to her in college, and I didn't blame her.

When I was in college, I had no home to go back to and decided to stay on campus in my apartment over a holiday weekend. My best friend asked her boyfriend who lived in the area to stay with me to keep me safe and help me with anything I needed. She was a good friend and the three of us (my best friend, her boyfriend and I) were all close, we hung out together all the time.

He took me out to dinner and when we got back to my apartment he forced himself on me. (Just because a man takes you to dinner doesn't automatically give him the right to have sex with you!) I said no, but I wasn't strong enough yet. I was carrying the shame of knowing my biological mother was a prostitute, which played out in my promiscuity. He persisted and I gave in. I know it's not entirely his fault. I was to blame too. I was the other person in the interaction. I allowed him to pressure me as part of a pattern of subservience that has played out in my life too many times. That wasn't the first time a man forced himself on me after I said NO and it wouldn't be the last. If it had happened now I would kick him in the nut sack and put him in a choke hold and that would be the end of it. In college I had no self esteem and was a lost mess.

Afterwards, I felt horrible. I told my friend what happened when she came over the next day but she knew already – she had a dream about it. That ended our friendship even though they stayed together – which really hurt me. I tried to get her back, I apologized numerous times in numerous ways, but she could not accept it.

It broke my heart but over time with all the healing work I did, I was able to forgive myself. I healed multiple imbalanced energies at once: betrayal, subservience, dominating male energy, guilt, shame.

You can imagine the shock when she called me out of the blue after nearly thirty years and I had just thought about her. She said she tracked me down and wanted to make amends, she was ready. I was in tears. Even though I already had forgiven myself, I felt like it completed the unresolved karmic energy between us. This was another gift and miracle and perfect timing to add to my sunflower because I know this is a common theme among women and this happens often. This is something that we individually need to heal and collectively support each other. **No means NO** – and that's that.

SOPHIEL "I am one with my emotions."

We are here nurturing you into the warming waters of the emotions unfelt, within the depths of your soul.

It is here that you begin to allow the waves of the Sophiel Light to soothe
your awareness within the wounds that have been encrusted and har-
bored from the light.

It is safe to feel the depth of shadow that has been distanced. It is safe to
allow the fluids of "afterbirth" to be seen. It is safe to sit in the waters of
tears unshed.

The Sophiel is the fluid light within all perceived darkness. It is the emotions that are the beauty and grace of being human.

It is the allowance to feel. It is the gift of feeling emotion.

It is the space where one can bathe and incubate within the womb of the Divine Mother's embrace.

Allow yourself to feel the arms of the Divine Mothers soothing you, holding space for you to feel, feel, feel, to purge, to weep, gently allowing the salted tears to birth new pathways for the light to burn away the encrusted shadow of karmas no longer.

Bathe Dear Sacred One, in the Light of the Holy Sophiel waters again and again and again.

The time is now to feel all unfelt.

Blessed are you Holy Light, Blessed are you.

HEAL HEAL HEAL

Receiving insight and wisdom from dreams is common for me. I do a lot of work while I slumber, a lot of healing on myself, and on others. As I was drifting off to sleep one night I heard: Then revealed and blended together.

This is what healing means to me. Once we've gone through the process of uncovering our traumas, wounds and self limiting beliefs by shining the light of consciousness on them, then feeling, processing, and purifying them, we can fully blend or integrate them into our being.

This is how we become whole.

If we take it high, the truth is we are already healed and whole. Keep that in the back of your mind when you are going through this process. There is a part of you, the greatest part-your divinity, that is healed, whole and complete already. We are just purifying and integrating the perceived wounds, karma, and imbalances of our human selves back to the light. **The wholeness lies beneath**.

It's easier to heal when you have the awareness that you are the one who created the obstacles, adversities and problems in the first place to enable your soul-growth. For me, at least it took the guilt out of the equation; therefore less charge, less shame, less attachment and easier to heal.

"We remind & assure you, that the 'purposed illusion' of Earthplane Life is about spiritual growth, about learning 'responsible co-creation in the 'University of Duality. The problems you encounter are chosen by your higher self, tailor made for you to grow! Indeed, it is often directly because of problems, that you humans grow mentally and spiritually. It is through the pain of confronting and resolving problems that you learn. It is not easy, but it is gratifying." ~Metatron

Worth repeating: It is through the pain of confronting and resolving problems that we learn. It is not easy, but it is gratifying once we get to the other side.

As the saying goes, 'You can pay me now, or pay me later.' You cannot evade your issues, you may delay them, but you will not transcend your issues, your problems, your chosen obstacles, until you confront and resolve them. So remember another saying: 'There is no time like the present!'

The time to be free is now, holy lights.

Until you truly face the self, you will not truly love or know the self. In self-realization, you learn to value yourself because you come to re-remember and know who you are- Holy Light of God incarnate. When you choose to awaken to your divinity within and do this inner work, you are left with a liberating presence of your authentic self that no one or no thing can ever replace.

REFLECT AND RESURRECT
BABY! NOW WE RISE

You are the chooser and the chosen, the creator and the created, the dreamer and the dream.

It's always good to look back for the sake of taking heed to how far you've come. But remember, don't look back and stay back. Use the past to learn from then move on. The only way we learn and grow is by experience.

***Clarity Above the Sea

Spirit gave me a new visualization. Feel free to use it if it calls to you.

I have come full circle again. Now I'm standing on top of a boulder that is rising out of the sea, glistening with the sea water, my arms outstretched, my heart open, receiving the sun. I am rooted on top of a boulder and I am free.

The waters that encircle the boulder represent the emotional aspects of creator light. From the vantage point as the observer I choose which emotions that I want to be able to swim and coalesce with. From this vantage point I am not entangled. I can see the full filmstrip in its past, present, and future forms. From this vantage point I can choose.

Waters are representative of my heart center, of my deep emotional threads. My emotional trajectory runs deep on earth. I have been on earth for many many lifetimes and many of them were extreme. When I rise into this new vantage point, into the space of the observer, I will be able to see and feel through the heart portal which is a space of clarity which is different from entangled emotion.

Now I swim up to the surface of the water and take a deep breath- breathe in the frequency of the new light of the new earth. No more being immersed in emotion under the water. where I lived much of my existence from the opposite end- arms outstretched looking at the surface, immersed in the polarity of thoughts and entangled emotion. Time to rise into the pinnacle point standing on the boulder, arms outstretched face reaching toward the heavens, sun beating down on my body where I am able to see with clarity through my heart center. I am free.

***Calming the Storm

One of the most challenging lessons I have had to learn besides being in control of my unstable mind is being in control of my emotions and that visualization was a great help to me. Although my first reaction was doubtful to be honest. Choosing my emotions was not something I thought I could do.

I don't know which one was more trying, controlling my thoughts or controlling my emotions! Not easy because:

1. I'm a woman, therefore emotional comes with the territory;
2. I'm a Pisces Sun/Scorpio Moon, all water which represents the emotions;
3. I have a lot of passion, ie., fire.

Be it as it may, I surprised myself. One day, just after I published my first book, my daughter was staying with me for a visit and we got into it, like we always did.

***Put the Plate Down

I lived in a small studio apartment in Long Island so there was not much space for another person, but she's my daughter so if I had been living in a cardboard box I'd make room for her. She started doing her "thing," pushing my buttons and the place seemed smaller as she spoke. I was not in a balanced place at the moment and I tried to communicate this to her. I had just walked in the door from doing errands with bags of stuff. I told her I was cranky and needed to eat and asked if we could talk later. She took this the wrong way, and no matter how hard I tried we still got into it, back and forth with the bickering.

I was trying really hard to remain calm and unaffected but when she took it to another level and said, "You're a hypocrite Mom. Just because you wrote a book doesn't mean you changed." Big trigger! I got so angry I reactivated my first impulse that was my old typical response. I was in the kitchen so I picked up a plate, cocked my arm back to throw it against the wall, but then something inside clicked and I put the plate down.

If anyone has been in a similar situation you know how hard it can be to walk away or actually stop an angry physical reaction when the energy is going in that direction. Anger is a very strong emotion. It takes so much will power and inner strength, but I knew that wasn't me anymore. I was really proud of myself. My daughter was still upset and lashed out at me some more and then locked herself in the pantry hysterically crying. I walked away and went into the other room to sit down calmly on the couch.

"Did I do thaaaaat?"

Just to make sure I was really walking my talk, the universe tested me again, that same day.

***Return to Sender

One of my closest and dearest sister friends called me and started vomiting her unhealed emotions on me over the phone about how angered she was about not getting credit for editing my book. She claimed that I didn't thank her anywhere. She said she didn't feel appreciated or seen by me and couldn't believe I hadn't even given her a free book. I was shocked. I was still on a high from the book signing and she was my biggest fan and cheerleader.

I tried to explain myself or rather defend myself, but it only made it worse. I got angry and raised my voice in defense. We got nowhere. We ended the call. I was deeply hurt. I couldn't believe this person who was like a mother to me, turned on me and dumped all her stuff on me. I went to the beach to go for a walk and just sat there and cried.

My inner wisdom knew it was not my stuff. I knew her so well and I knew exactly where her hurt was coming from. It wasn't about ME because she was the only person I HAD thanked twice in my book. Even with that knowledge, it felt like a betrayal. It must have been "dump your garbage out on Soulfire Day."

I paused and thought about what I can do with all this conflicting energy. I closed my eyes, took a deep breath and asked God and spirit to take away the anguish I felt in my heart. It wasn't mine and I knew it. I took a deep breath and wahlla! it was gone, just like that. It was amazing!

It took many years of spiritual training to get to this point. My new way of being didn't happen overnight. I have been working on myself for nearly two decades! But I proved to myself that change can happen. You can be the calm in the chaos. You can remain the lighthouse, the steady pillar of strength. It is possible. I'm a very emotional being. I had to work hard on self-control to get to this point of getting control over my emotions. So if I can do it, so can you.

It also helps if you have the awareness when other people are dumping their toxic crap on you and it's not yours to own or take in. Just put your hand up to block their energy and say, "No thank you, return to sender." To remain calm when someone is attacking you is one of the greatest feats one can achieve.

When we tend to our own spiritual garden, we then have the fortitude to be the light for others. Someone's gotta stay awake and vigilant! In this way we care for ourselves and our own corner of the universe and light up the world. We must release the violence from our own hearts if we sincerely want to have peace and harmony in the world.

***08-08 The Lions Gate

Another memorable shift happened with my Hawaiian Beloved. I reached out to him to talk about our kitty and he responded to me in victim mode, saying, "My heart is destroyed, I'm alone, struggling and I want to give up."

I felt the negative energies go right into my gut. I felt sick to my stomach again, right back where I had been trying to heal from our break up. The rest of the day I moped around, no energy, feeling down and feeling all sorts of emotions: mostly guilt and sadness.

On Karma's evening walk, the nature, the elementals and my higher self communicated with me. Hawaii was working her magic, making it hard for me to stay in a bad mood. As I was walking Karma I observed the amazing beauty all around me. I gave thanks to the Aina and this magical land. I realized I was living my dream life that I had worked hard, so hard to create. I was tired of feeling sad and bad. No more! I'm not going down that road again, especially when it's not my stuff. It was HB's stuff to work out. I am not responsible for his happiness or anyone else's.

"I am not wasting one more second of my beautiful dream life feeling bad and sad."I declared cutting the air. As soon as I did, I felt the heavy emotions leave my gut and my body. I felt light again. I continued, "I choose my emotions and I choose to be happy." And so it is. AHO.

It was an amazing shift and it lasted. I went to bed feeling proud of myself, acknowledging the huge accomplishment. I think that praising yourself is another component that is crucial in self-love, healing and evolution. We praise our closest friend, so we should do this for ourselves. We must become our closest and dearest friend and our greatest cheerleader. Acknowledge your small victories.

I am the chooser of my emotions.

***Tsunami Soulfire

Then there's this...There were many times when I had no control of my emotions when I was with my HB. One particular moment stands out as the tsunami of all Soulfire tsunamis. It was Christmas time 2020 and we were back at his cabin hoping to spend a nice time together without fighting.

Even though we both had the same intention, there were higher forces at work. He and I were going at it, over something little. You know how those arguments start, they're really not about the half and half but something deeper. This argument escalated from cream for coffee to everything that was wrong with each other. Our pain bodies were in full activation!

When I got out of control and was too loud for him, his pattern was to say, "This conversation is over. I'm done." and clam up. That would only make me even more furious because I wasn't done speaking and he was being controlling and shutting me down. I hated that reaction with every ounce of my being. What was even worse was when he yelled at me to shut up. I went into a rage like the female version of the Incredible Hulk. I had no control of my emotions, all I could see in my vision was red, literally. I was screaming things at him that I don't even know what I said.

It felt like I was screaming and yelling for all the Me's, in all my timelines, in all my incarnations that were subservient. For all the times a man told me to shut up, stifled my voice, stuck me in a dark room, and diminished my light. I was like a fire breathing dragon. At that moment I knew it too! I knew I was going to clear some heavy duty karma and archetypes, it was time and I had the awareness in the back of my mind. Shush me no more! It was ugly, but necessary.

Later, when the storm calmed I apologized to him and tried to make amends. It always seemed like I was the first and sometimes only one to apologize. He accepted my apology but withheld his affection toward me for the rest of the trip. While I understood, it still hurt me to the core. That is not something I can handle too well.

There was a silver lining in this Soulfire Tsunami. The explosion led me to help me heal the timelines that were still alive wire in my Akash. Again, he was the catalyst to my deep deep healing.

***Healing the Akash

Right after that outburst I woke up in the middle of the night, bolted straight up in bed, heart pounding with fear and anxiety as I sat in the dark. I said to myself, "I'm here again." I knew deep down that something was not right. It was a week later when I learned about the active timelines that needed healing.

I came to learn that I was healing four timelines at once with my HB: ours and three others. When will it end!

When I learned about the three other timelines that were still active in my Akash, (book of life) it made sense and I understood myself better. In the first timeline, I gave all of myself to a man I loved. He in turn locked me in a dark room and kept me a secret because he had another family and life. I was reliving this out now with my HB, not that he locked me in a dark room, but aspects of the patterns from that timeline were bleeding over.

In the second timeline, I was a famous healer in the far east trained by a master healer. He put me behind glass on display and stood behind me as I did healings. When he didn't like my interaction with a man he secretly took away my healing powers. I did not know he was taking away my power so I started to doubt myself and my healing abilities. I finally understood why I carried so much self-doubt when I began to become an energy healer in this lifetime.

In the third timeline, I was a genius mathematical savant and had notebooks of equations that would help heal the world. I lived in an era when women were suppressed and had no voice. A man in my religious community knew about my notebooks and came to my library demanding I give them to him. When I refused he took out a knife, slit my throat and killed me. Thanks.

What do all the timelines have in common? The same karmic patterns I brought into this life: subservience, allowing others to control me, allowing people to manipulate me and diminish my light, self-doubt, taking the blame, second guessing myself and believing that it was my fault because that is what unhealed mirrors project upon you.

Many of us are clearing ancestral traumas and patterns that have been carried for lifetimes and centuries. The trauma is stored within our cellular memories, as well as around us in our aura as negative persistent thoughts. This is important to be aware of when you start doing this type of work/healing. It can be exhausting. Be gentle and extra kind to yourself.

I learned how to heal these active timelines by sitting with each one, feeling her/my pain, mourning, then when I felt ready, re-writing a new ending with pen to paper. It was profound. I spent the first part of 2021 doing this inner work. The last timeline I healed was the one with the relationship with my Hawaiian Beloved, and it was the hardest.

"If the illusion of 3D did not feel real, you would not learn. Indeed the pains you feel, the joys you experience, are real...and serve your growth

& expansion. Masters, nothing is final, all is dynamic! Each of you can change the past as well as the future. That is why when we work with the Akash and rewrite our stories/incarnations we change the past. Because the highest truth is Time does not exist in linear time. In the multi-verse there is only Now moment, so it is possible to change your past." ~Metatron

NOTHING IS SET IN STONE, ALL IS CHANGING AND DYNAMIC, ESPECIALLY YOU.

Change and rebirth are not always pretty, in fact it's ugly, messy, painful, and scary. It's ok if you have these reactions. Try not to judge yourself. This doesn't mean it's ok to go around screaming and yelling and

unleashing your anger on others. Sometimes it happens and sometimes it can be a very powerful wake up call. Anger is a strong emotion- used for good it can be the catalyst for change.

Individually and collectively women are going through a massive re-birth. We have been silent, our voices stifled, our lights diminished, our talents gone unheard for way too long. This is the time of the awakening of the divine feminine- not in a bitchy way, but in a kind, caring, fierce and powerful way. We are becoming nurturing warriors and the lights of the world. There is no stopping the divine feminine.

***Karma is No Joke

My dog Karma reminds me of the power of the divine feminine. Although she is part Weiner dog and only 30 lbs, she is a force to be reckoned with. She exhibits the protective nurturing warrior spirit in the body of a little hot dog.

One day, Karma and I were walking at the harbor in Hawaii. I had my daughter's pup, Lotus, on a leash, and Karma was walking freely. Karma is usually attached to my hip so I trust her to stay next to me.

Out of the blue, my eleven year old little Karma started running fero-ciously barking toward a man and his dog who were walking about one hundred feet away. I ran after her screaming because when I looked closely I realized the other dog was a pit bull. Karma had been attacked once by a pit bull and nearly died, so I was freaking out. Thank God the other dog was on a leash.

When I finally got to her, I apologized to the man. He said, "No problem, my dog is an asshole." That's what he said. Karma must have sensed the asshole dog from afar and was running to protect us. I couldn't believe it. She would have risked her life to protect us. This little dog is so loyal and fearless. I love her more than life.

Another incident displaying Karma's true nature, happened in Long Island at a dog park that we frequented. We arrived around sunset and no one else was there, which was unusual for this busy dog park, except for two men in hoodies sitting on top of the table at the entrance to the nature trail. I parked away from the two strange men. When I got out of the car the men immediately started walking toward us. All the hair on my body was standing at attention, Karma must have felt the energy because she started going crazy. I had never seen that side of Karma before, growling and showing her teeth like she was ready to tear them apart. It didn't stop them, as they got closer she started lunging at them now, ready to bite. Luckily I had her on leash. Something was wrong and we both felt it.

They came right up to us and said, "Do you want to go for a walk?"

What! Are you kidding, I'm thinking, Sure, so you can rape me and chop me up into little pieces and bury me? Of course I didn't say that. I showed no fear and said nonchalantly, "No thanks," and walked away with my keys between my knuckles ready to defend myself and Karma if necessary.

I walked briskly to my car with eyes in the back of my head. I showed no alarm so they didn't sense my internal fear. Something I learned about this type of situation, show no fear, otherwise they will be more tempted to assert their power over you.

No time to be scared while I walked, but when I got in my car I kind of freaked out. My heart was beating so fast! I had avoided something really sinister I felt. I was so grateful to Karma. I knew she would have defended me with her life. I just hope that never happens.

Can you imagine if all the women in the world started to be like Karma? Protecting the babies and the children. Fearless, loyal, protective and 100% warrior. That is the divine feminine energy. Some might think of it as weak, but it is the opposite. The divine feminine is rooted in strength and conviction- rooted in her knowing and the divine power.

Why do you think we refer to nature as Mother Nature? Why is our beloved planet earth, Gaia, feminine? Because Mother/Woman is the most powerful force on the planet. Wild and unpredictable, yet nurturing, loving, and providing at the same time. That's the energy I want to embrace, the nurturing warrior light, free from entanglements.

Spirit gave me another visualization, this was my first one as earth. They showed me as a tree trunk, a pillar of light, rising up from the crystalline grid of Gaia, with branches free, not entangled with other branches-blossoming their own flowers. I love this one because I feel so connected to the trees and Gaia and it reminds me to avoid the toxic entanglements of others.

ROOTED CLARITY ROOTED CLARITY ROOTED CLARITY UNITY IS THE ONE.

It is from this space we can build anew, a new life, a new earth, built on the foundation of wholeness and unity without entanglements and that was key for me to embrace. This was a new definition of unity for me. I never thought of unity like that, but it makes sense. Unity is found within and is not entangled. I love the metaphor of Unity as a candle that ignites the light of others without entanglement. Unity is a pillar of light burning brightly on its own.

***New VF

The latest logo of my unfolding came to me when my guides told me I had "leveled up" to a new vibrational frequency. My current imprint is a Galactic sunflower with a lighthouse in the middle, shining five light beams of sacred geometry representing the five modalities I offer:

* Spoken Word
* Written Word
* Movement with Breath
* Connection to the Masses
* Working One on One

I love how the sunflower, which is me, has transformed into a galactic one now. As I evolve in my consciousness I become more and more of my multi dimensional galactic Self and at the same time realize there is so much more of me and the multiverse to explore and discover. This is the fun part now. I have made it through the density and polarity, now I am free to adventure deeper within and higher withup.

I am this beacon of unfiltered light rooted firmly in mother earth, shining brightly to all the souls on the sea guiding them back home. Our destiny is to rise into the spectacular light beings that we already are. To heal the hole and become whole once again. That is why taking time to make yourself the priority and spending time doing the inner work is not a selfish act. We are all connected, so when you heal yourself the entire planet is uplifted to a new vibrational resonance. You actually change the crystalline grid of Gaia. Every soul matters, every soul is an integral part in the ocean of divinity. Heal the Hole, Heal the Whole.

What is your Kuleana? (Responsibility)

This might not be completely accurate but you get the point...

  *One individual who lives and vibrates to the energy of optimism and a willingness to be nonjudgmental of others will counterbalance the negativity of 90,000 individuals who calibrate at the lower weakening levels.
  *One individual who lives and vibrates to the energy of pure love and reverence for all of life will counterbalance the negativity of 750,000 individuals who calibrate at the lower weakening levels.
  *One individual who lives and vibrates to the energy of illumination, bliss, and infinite peace will counterbalance the negativity of 10 million people who calibrate at the lower weakening levels.
  *One individual who lives and vibrates to the energy of grace, pure spirit beyond the body, in a world of complete oneness, will counterbalance the negativity of 70 million people who calibrate at the lower weakening levels. (From Kate Earthsong)

Alchemical Tools

***The Doorway to Grace: Gratitude

THERE'S NO MAGIC FORMULA OR pill for change, at least not yet! It takes persistent consistent effort and discipline. It helps to identify your triggers. It helps to practice self-care. It helps to have support, someone to share your journey with so you remember you are not alone and what you're going through many other souls are going through. It helps to relax more, to breathe more, to smile more. It helps to count your blessings and stay in an attitude of gratitude.

If there ever was a magic spell I'd say it would be gratitude. It's a magic feeling-the doorway to grace. Why? For the simple fact that it opens your heart. It's hard to keep your heart closed, when you acknowledge the blessings and notice all the beauty and abundance around you. You can't help but have an open heart. Try it next time. Start to feel what an open heart feels like.

An open heart is not some whimsical romantic notion to attract a mate, it is the key to everything as a spiritual being having this human experience. When you live from the heart frequency and your pure resonance you can restructure your reality based on joy, truth, and all that is meaningful for you. Your heart is where your power lies.

I like to take Karma for a walk in the morning and do a walking gratitude meditation. As I'm walking, I just say "thank you" to everything I observe. "Good morning tree, thank you for your oxygen. Thank you Plumeria for smelling so good. Thank you earth for supporting me. Thank you beautiful flowers for adding your colors to the world. Thank you birds for your song. Thank you grass for unconditional love, thank you sky and all your beautiful shades of blue, thank you clouds for your shade, thank you sun for giving me life and healing, thank you air for your sweet smell and pure energy, thank you ocean…I love you so much." As you are doing this you will feel your heart opening and your body relaxing. You will be vibrating at a very high frequency-the highest.

The beautiful thing about opening your heart and raising your VF is that you don't need money to do this. You don't need a college degree or even a high school diploma. You don't need a fancy car or house or anything for that matter. Anyone can do this. This is the key to your salvation. This practice brings you in the present moment full of grace, humbleness, and gratitude- all the traits of God, which is you. You feel lighter and become the light when you relax, breathe deeply and open your heart. This is you at your finest, your God self comes alive with this practice and your light will send off a beacon so bright it will beam through the darkness across the universe to be seen and felt by the angels.

Besides this walking gratitude meditation I try to bring that same energy and awareness into my everyday life and not take for granted one day that I am alive. I make it a practice and habit to acknowledge and admire the beauty and abundance that is all around and not become too busy in my head and life to see the amazing gift and miracle that we have been bestowed.

***Healing Relationship Rifts in your Sleep

Sometimes disagreements between two people cannot come to a mutual understanding and be resolved in the 3D plane. Either one or both are stuck in seeing the situation only through their lens and not being open to really listening or communing with the other. This happens all the time with all types of relationships. Instead of leaving unresolved negative energies in the relationship to fester, there is something you can do without their conscious participation.

I learned through painful soulmate breakups that the best thing you can do is communicate with them on a higher level, in other words, your higher self communicates with their higher self, expressing honestly how you feel, asking for harmony and peace in the relationship, blessing them and letting them go. It's powerful and effective. The reason it works is because there is a vibrational reality where part of us exists. If peace and harmony exists in that reality, then eventually it will filter down into the 3D reality we experience on the earth plane.

Sometimes you get confirmation through a dream that all is resolved like I did with a client. I had been working one on one with clients for twenty years and always have had great communication, mutual understanding and respect with all my clients. I love my clients, they are like family to me.

I had a misunderstanding and miscommunication about payment for a session with a client. We were both upset with each other and he let me go through a very unpleasant text. Instead of getting angry I tried to stay in a place of understanding and peace. He was one of my favorite clients. He loved yoga so much he even turned his basement into a beautiful yoga studio. Yoga saved his dental practice. Those were the things I focused on, not the misunderstanding. He hadn't paid for the last canceled session, and I didn't want the money because I felt it would carry bad energy with it. But my wise friend told me I had to take it, otherwise there would be imbalanced karma between us. That resonated as true for me so I texted him my address. (I have very wise friends).

In the interim I had a dream I was giving him a yoga session and he was so happy and grateful for me. After the session he wrote me a check with a big smile on his face and inscribed something on it. I didn't read it. I just took the check from him, folded it in half, put it in my purse and said thank you. Then I left. It was our last session and I was saying goodbye.

I woke up feeling so good about that dream. It showed me that in another dimension, in another vibrational reality, that all was healed and forgiven. I received the actual check shortly after that. Karma balanced, harmony restored. I had done the work and it paid off.

I often remind myself that I have to walk my talk-that it is everything to me. Luckily, I have had A LOT of practice with this!

***Ho'oponopono

Another wonderful spiritual tool is Ho'oponopono, an ancient Hawaiian healing practice that brings balance and harmony back to your innate wholeness. Ho'o means "to make" and pono means "right", so ho'oponopono translates into "to make rightly right."

While the traditional method involves many different steps and processes, the modern version has been simplified down to just four steps. These steps involve meditating, reflecting and chanting of four simple mantras:

* I am sorry
* Please forgive me
* Thank you
* I love you

Ho'oponopono first gained attention when Dr. Ihaleakala Hew Len used the method to cure criminally insane patients without confronting them or talking to them once. Instead, he focused his attention on each patient while reciting the mantras. Remarkably, the patients began to be cured and his work became famous all over the world. In fact, his cure rate was so high that the particular ward of the Hawaii State hospital ended up closing down.

According to Dr. Ihaleakala Hew Len, he healed these patients by working on himself. He asked himself- "What is going on in me that I am creating this experience?" And then used the mantras to clear and release the shared "data" or karma he had with these patients. The nice thing about this practice is that you don't have to know exactly what the karma or shared 'data' is for it to be cleared.

We are all one and we are all responsible for the world we are creating. Most of us are doing it unconsciously, but we are still doing it. Consensus reality is a term that refers to the collective reality. Collectively, we create the world that we live in and we draw experiences into our lives that help us grow and mirror what we need to learn.

By taking responsibility for everything that comes our way, and clearing it through forgiveness and love, we can clear the "data" that is playing out in our subconscious and change how we experience or perceive other people and the world around us. As Dr. Len states, "If I see you as being crazy, it is only my experience of you, so if I clear that, I can no longer see you as that." By forgiving and loving himself and these patients, he was able to bring healing to them and himself.

I love this perspective. When I'm doing healings with someone I visualize them as already healed. I don't see the injury or the trauma, I see them as light, whole and perfect. That is how Jesus healed the lepers. He was not afraid of them. He saw them in their true Godly state of health and well being. If you can hold that vision and believe it, miracles happen.

The beauty of Ho'oponopono is that the other person doesn't need to be involved. You are "clearing the air" energetically. You can simply do it on your own and receive all the healing benefits. This is what I have been practicing with my Hawaiian Beloved. I also used this tool when I was living with my imbalanced landlord, M. It helps so much.

Ho'oponopono is a fantastic healing tool for:

* Clearing karmic ties/past life issues with another person
* Healing relationships
* Finding peace with a loved one who has passed
* Mending family connections
* Clearing energy with anyone

Here's how to practice: First, think about the person and the relationship that needs healing. Visualize them in your mind, but know that when you are doing this work, it is truly about you. The other person is just a mirror to access the part of you that needs to be healed.

1. **"I am Sorry"** Apologize to the person for anything and everything. This step is about taking responsibility for your involvement and your

energy that contributed to the situation. You may have not caused the situation, but you are responsible for the situation now that it is in your life. By saying you are sorry, you start to clear away the karmic or energetic patterns or ties that may have brought this situation into your life.

2. **"Please Forgive Me"** Now that you have apologized, ask for forgiveness. This is about forgiving yourself, so you can clear the energy between you and the other person, or the situation. Allow yourself to feel that forgiveness has been granted to you, no matter what you have done.

3. **"Thank You"** Thank the person not just for forgiving you but for everything. Thank them for the contribution they made to your life and the lessons they have taught you. Thank them for being a part of your life. Thank them for revealing this part of you, and for giving you this opportunity to heal this energy. Thank yourself too, for taking this step and for allowing yourself to be healed.

4. **"I Love You"** This step is about honoring their soul, the deeper part of them that is just like you. Depending on your relationship with the person, this step may be the hardest, but try your best to open your heart and find a way to genuinely send love to this person. Say the words, "I love you." Loving a person doesn't mean you have to like them or even agree with them. It's a form of agape love, which is the highest non personal unconditional love or charity for all.

As you recite the mantras, you are healing yourself even though you are directing the energy towards the other person. Oneness is real.

You can also do this practice toward yourself. You can direct it to the inner wounded child or any age that you need repairing from trauma. It will help you heal and return the fragments of your being back to wholeness.

***Sacred Dance

It's easy to get caught up in circumstance, it's even easier to break out in a dance! Everything is energy. Sometimes it builds up in the body and auric field and we just need to release it and shake it loose. I find putting on my happy playlist and dancing freely, losing myself in the moment and in the music is like a healing balm for my body, mind and soul. When I dance it's an offering, a prayer and dedication to God, Gaia, to my ancestors, to All.

I get the God bumps all over my body and that's when I know I'm back! The anxiety leaves and I am back to my peaceful centered Self. It only takes but a minute.

> When you're in your mind and in the doubt, dance it out.
> When you're in a rut and you're really stuck,
> dance it out.
> When you've lost your groove and your booty won't
> move, dance it out.

If you absolutely don't want to dance, get up and do jumping jacks, go for a run or walk. As long as you do something to move your body while breathing deeply, you will release energy buildup.

Badass Humans

***Two Legged's vs. Four

I BUMPED INTO A MAN that I had met before at the vet. His dog had some health issues. He told me his dog passed away but the good thing was that his dog did it playing and running – he was happy. He followed it up with, "I still haven't met a two legged that gives that same unconditional love."

I get it. I really do. Being a dog owner myself and on the receiving end of my soul joy, Karma's unconditional love, I knew what he meant. I used to say the same thing. However, if you want unconditional love you must become unconditional love for yourself. You can't get what you can't give. You must become the beloved of your own heart first.

This is a common phenomena. When people disappoint, we turn to the animal kingdom for a source of love. Even more common is focusing all of our attention and sourcing our love and happiness from our children and forgetting about ourselves. This creates an unhealthy imbalance in the relationship. I agree with Carl Jung that the greatest tragedy of the family is the unlived lives of the parents. You have to find it within first, or you will always have a void. Our children mirror us. They do what we do, not what we say. I learned this first hand from my daughter. The best thing we can do for our kids is to become the beloved of our own heart.

I speak from experience. I recently received this message from my daughter when I couldn't attend her graduation from Culinary School in Manhattan:

"Aww it's okay that's what I figured! You are forever in my heart and with me in spirit, so I'm not sad. I know you have to take care of the life you've been building!

You inspire me Mama. You are the reason I am where I am! You taught me how to be determined, compassionate, spiritually grounded, independent and self sufficient while balancing being open enough to receive. You gave me the option to explore what and who I wanted to be and never forced me even if you didn't always agree with what I wanted to do. I am grateful for all the lessons that you taught me that made me a wise, skillful, creative human being.

You were the best teacher of unconditional love! All while healing your own trauma you showed up for me and made sure I was well taken care of always. I love you! Thank you for all the hard days and sacrifices you put in for 28+ years."

"Well done," the angels say. I agree, "Well done."

From above in the celestial realms it is an honor to be a mother here on earth. I am honored to be a mother to a beautiful spirited child. She makes me so proud. And not because of what she has accomplished, which is so much in her short lifespan, but who she has become- the kindness, generosity, mercy and charity she holds in her heart and shares with others. I just wanted her to be a kind person to everyone and she has become that pure heart.

If you read my memoir, *Fearless,* you know of the struggles I had with raising her as my daughter. She was stubborn, strong willed, and had her own opinion about everything at the age of two. We were in constant power struggles and battles, but we made it through. On May 15, 2019 at the age of 26 I heard the words, "You're right Mom," come out of her mouth for the first time. I made May 15th the "You're Right Mom" holiday. It's even better than Mother's Day to me! Please feel free to use it for yourself.

***Happy

My daughter, being the beautiful precious light she is, took to the song, *Happy* by Pharell. When it first came out, she told me to download it and listen to it, that it was amazing. I followed her advice and I hated the song. I thought it was completely annoying. It stayed a part of my ITunes library, but I never listened to it again, and if I heard it on the radio I immediately changed the channel.

A few years later I had a dream about the song. I was a teacher discussing with a few of my students about how the song, *Happy,* is a reflection of our innermost being. One student was commenting how he didn't like the song and another one was totally digging it. It seems that you either hate the song or love it, there's really no in-between.

I shared with the students in my dream how much the song irritated me when it first came out. Then unexpectedly, about two years later I heard it again and had a completely different reaction. I listened and sang along and danced with pure delight.

Now *Happy* is on my Soulfire's Happy playlist along with my other favorites.

So what changed??? Obviously not the song. I think this song is a perfect reflection of "the outer is a reflection of the inner." Maybe all the work I had been doing on myself was paying off? Maybe I am happy after all?!

Becoming happy is not a selfish act. It is just the opposite, it is the most glorious act of giving you can do for yourself, the people around you and the collective. Being truly happy is being light and light is God. Don't we need more light in the world? Amen.

***Captain John

Maybe I should have shared Happy with Captain John. He was a neighbor in Long Island who was a jaded ex-cop/alcoholic that drove an old beat up dirty van filled with empty McDonalds bags. We were an unlikely match for conversation, but I had a soft spot in my heart for Captain John. He reminded me of my Dad in a way, maybe because he was an alcoholic Irishman.

While walking Karma through the neighborhood, he would stop his van and always ask me the same two questions: "Let me ask you something," he'd start with, "Did you watch the news today?" I'd respond, "No I don't

watch the news." He continued anyway, "Who do you think is better...
animals or humans?" Sometimes the conversation would continue. I
would try to cheer him up with positive news and give him some hope
for humanity. I even gave him one of my inspirational yoga calendars
one year. That wasn't enough for Captain John though. He had already
determined that the world was a cruel and harsh place, and I understood where he was coming from. I heard him one day in his backyard
screaming and crying out in pain like a wounded animal. It was heartbreaking to listen to. He passed away around the same time as my father.
I miss him.

Sadly, many people I know feel the same way. I hear it all the time,
"People suck. Animals are better." I get it, I do. But we can't give up on
people. I still believe in the goodness of people. I believe that for every
sucky person in the world, there are at least one hundred or more good
people. The news doesn't highlight the small kind deeds that are being
done all over the world by millions of good people. The news focuses
on creating fear based mind control and propaganda and lies to keep
you un-empowered. My advice to Captain John should have been to stop
watching the news. Maybe he would have attracted one of the good people into his life?

***Hawaiiana & Nepali

If Captain John knew the people from Hawaii and Nepal I think his
opinion of humans would have changed. One thing I learned in
Hawaii very quickly was how resilient and strong the people are. Local
after local that I spoke with, told me their story of such complete
heartbreak and loss, yet they still carry on with a smile on their face,
the Aloha spirit in their heart, and Pono in their doing. These people
are hard core. I am blown away and have such respect for them. I have
met the kindest, most giving people in Hawaii with the true spirit of
Aloha.

The Hawaiian people remind me of the people I met in Nepal. They are from the same mold. In Nepal they have nothing, it is a very poor country. But they are happy and they shine with the light of God through their eyes. They are some of the most beautiful, kind, giving people I have ever met.

The people of Nepal don't get cranky when the power is out, and there is no water or Wifi. They just keep steady and smiling. It is really a trait I admire. Yoga philosophy calls this "Stiirham Sukham," which means steady and happy, which the people of Nepal completely embrace.

The traditional tantric yoga I learned from my pilgrimage in Nepal was wonderful, but what left a lasting impression on my heart was the spirit of the people, especially the children! The children stole my heart. The children were the lights of God, just happy to be alive. The day we were leaving I cried blubbering out loud in front of everyone (I never cry in front of people). I just loved the people of Nepal so much. They have God in their heart and it shows.

> "What lies behind us and what lies before us are small matters compared to what lies within us. And when we bring what is within us out into the world, miracles happen." ~ Ralph Waldo Emerson

***You are the Miracle

So many seekers are waiting for someone to come save them, whether it's their Mom or Dad, Jesus or the ET aliens. We don't need saving. Humans have survived incredible hardships and are the most resilient, strong, powerful, courageous and compassionate beings that exist.

We plod through life suffering, experiencing heartbreak and after heartbreak, carrying our losses and griefs on our hearts, and the weight of the world on our shoulders, yet still manage to live and smile and be kind and help others and muster the courage to move forward despite adversities. If that is not saying something about the human spirit then I don't know what does. Humans are the bravest, most badass souls in all the multiverse.

The problem is we don't see ourselves in this way. We are not walking around with a mirror in front of us. We are encapsulated in our suffering and grief so much that we become defensive and closed, thinking there's something wrong with us. But there's nothing wrong with you. What's wrong is the world. You are perfect, powerful, holy and divine. You just forgot.

> I believe the greatest and deepest pain is the pain of not knowing your True self.

***Letting Go of the Past

I lost all my photos, photo albums and scrapbooks while I was here in Hawaii. All of my memories from when I was a little girl up until now were destroyed in a flood in a friend's basement back in Long Island where I was storing them. That was tough for me. I'm very sentimental and keep everything of meaning. I had thousands of photos. It was hard to let them go, but I had no choice. I had to accept my past being washed away in a flood. That is not as nearly as bad as the stories of some of the people I met here that had a more drastic purging with Pele's last lava flow in 2018. They lost everything, I mean every little material thing they owned, from their house to their photos. Pele destroyed it all. Do you know what grows abundantly out of the lava? The Ohi'a flower. Where lava flows, these amazing little flowers grow. Just because the Ohi'a lehua flower looks dainty and delicate, the plant itself is incredibly durable and can grow in rugged, barren environments.

This flower reminds me of the human spirit.

ALOHA

Just as the Ohi'a flower reflects the human spirit of perseverance and power so does the word, Aloha. Aloha has so many different meanings, like the Hindu word, Namaste, which is the traditional greeting in India and Nepal. Namaste means basically the light (divine) in me, see and honors that same light (divine) in you. It is a sacred greeting that keeps God alive in us. You bring your hands to prayer over your sacred heart center when you do this.

Aloha means hello and good-bye, which is symbolic of the cyclical nature of life. It also means love. In the Hawaiian of old, Aloha means "God in us."

When we break Aloha down it can mean the presence of the divine breath.

Alo means presence
Ha means breath
Non locals in Hawaii are referred to often as "Howlies," which means, without breath.

The traditional Hawaiian greeting is special and sacred. It is done with foreheads touching and sharing breath – which is sharing the presence of God. It is so beautiful to watch and also to do.

***Sharing Breath with the Honu

I had the opportunity to partake in this greeting before the C, social distancing and face suffocators. I also shared this greeting with a Honu that swam with me one day at Magic Sands Beach. The Honu and I were under water together just frolicking around when I ran out of air- still a problem! I came up to breathe and the Honu came up as well facing me just a couple of feet away. She opened her mouth and exhaled into my face. I was a bit taken aback. I was not expecting that! Boy did she have bad breath! But it was an honor and I felt blessed. We shared the breath of the divine in the ocean together, forever bonded.

Aloha is also defined as an acronym. Inspired by Maui elder and linguist Pilahi Paki's impassioned speech to community leaders, the law (Hawaii Revised Statutes, section 5-7.5) was passed in 1986:

"Akahai, meaning kindness, to be expressed with tenderness; Lōkahi, meaning unity, to be expressed with harmony; 'Olu'olu, meaning agreeable, to be expressed with pleasantness; Ha'aha'a, meaning humility, to be expressed with modesty; Ahonui, meaning patience, to be expressed with perseverance."

Pilahi Paki spoke of aloha not only as a definition, but as the legacy of Hawaii and its ancestors. Aloha embodies deeply held Hawaiian cultural beliefs about community, peace, spiritual truth, and expresses Hawaii's hopes for a harmonious future that extends to the whole world. The law continues,

"'Aloha' is more than a word of greeting or farewell or a salutation. 'Aloha' means mutual regard and affection and extends warmth in caring with no obligation in return. 'Aloha' is the essence of relationships in which each person is important to every other person for collective existence. 'Aloha' means to hear what is not said, to see what cannot be seen and to know the unknowable." Below are the words of Hawai'i's last reigning monarch, Queen Lili'uokalani (1891-93), containing the true meaning of the magical word:

"And wherever [the native Hawaiian] went he said 'Aloha' in meeting or in parting. 'Aloha' was a recognition of life in another. If there was life there was mana, goodness and wisdom, and if there was goodness and wisdom there was a god-quality. One had to recognize the 'god of life' in another before saying 'Aloha,' but this was easy. Life was everywhere – in the trees, the flowers, the ocean, the fish, the birds, the pili grass, the rainbow, the rock – in all the world was life–was god–was Aloha. Aloha in its gaiety, joy, happiness, abundance. Because of Aloha, one gave without thought of return; because of Aloha, one had mana. Aloha had its own mana. It never left the giver but flowed freely and continuously between giver and receiver. 'Aloha' could not be thoughtlessly or indiscriminately spoken, for it carried its own power. No Hawaiian could greet another with 'Aloha' unless he felt it in his own heart. If he felt anger or hate in his heart he had to cleanse himself before he said 'Aloha'."

The spirit of aloha is a way of life.

Can you see how rich and all encompassing this simple little word is. I say Aloha to almost everyone I see. Sadly, it's not heard too much here anymore, but I strive to keep the word, the energy and the tradition alive.

I created a new word: Alohaste. Alo-ha-stay
(Aloha and Namaste)

***Decisions, decisions, decisions

It appears we have some work cut out for us, but the only option is to not try and remain asleep, stagnant, and numb while we are alive. And what is the point of that? You might as well be dead. At least in death we are reunited with the totality of our being. Remember we chose to be here now. We each raised our hands and said "pick me, pick me!" Go out and live your own beautiful adventure. The greatest adventure however, is the discovery of you!

"People travel to wonder at the height of the mountains,
at the huge waves of the seas,
at the long course of the rivers,
at the vast compass of the ocean,
at the circular motion of the stars,
and yet they pass by themselves without wondering."
~ Saint Augustine

Make a commitment to yourself and your healing. You have to become selfish. You need to be selfish. Helping everyone else and ignoring yourself or putting yourself last is not loving yourself. This is the opposite of being your own beloved. It is a feeling of not being whole inside so in order to fill that void you do for everyone else so they can appreciate and need you. You have to make a decision and stick to it that your well being and awakening is your number one priority. A decision is a powerful force. Self imposed indecision brings frustration because it slows the process of creation down- dilutes the power of it.

I've learned I'm really good at making big decisions almost instantly. I knew I had to heal myself: body, mind and soul. I committed 100% and did it. I knew I had to resign from the bank as a financial consultant or my soul would wither up and die. I resigned without hesitation. I knew I wanted to move to Hawaii, and I did. What I falter with are the little decisions about things like what food to order from the menu, which dress to buy, which curtains go better in my bedroom, etc. That's ok.

***Plan F

Living in Hawaii had been a dream in my heart since I first visited back in 2000, but I didn't know how it would happen with no money (still harboring lack mentality then). I had plans though and quite a few.

I went through the different plans in my head:

Plan A...The universe sends me a big fat check out of the blue

Plan B...I receive a check from my worthless stock and mutual fund investment that miraculously took a turn for the better

Plan C...I receive a big settlement from the useless class action lawsuit I am a part of

Plan D...I can always live with Dreaming Bear and my daughter (Wait, they broke up and she's moving out)

Plan E…I manifest a work exchange at the most perfect space and I don't have to pay rent (but I'd have to share a bathroom)

Unfortunately, plan A fell through then plan B and plan C were all a bust. Even plan D and E fell through. So I went to plan F. You know what that was? FUCK IT, I'M GOING.

Plan F…FUCK IT
Plan G…Just GO!!!

And you know what? I didn't die. Yes, I had hard times and questioned the move. I even thought about going back to my old life that I was familiar with. I was frustrated at times, A LOT. But I stuck it out and I'm so happy now.

"Trust your inner voice. If you don't feel it, don't do it.
When you trust the wisdom within, the universe moves
mountains on your behalf." ~Sita

You might have a dream in your heart but think it's impossible to achieve. It's overwhelming so you procrastinate and stay in your daily routine which is safe. In this current era on earth we have the opportunity to re-create ourselves anew because all of our daily routines have been majorly disrupted.

Does a big bonfire start out as a big bonfire? Nope. It starts with one small flame. Flicker by flicker, flame by flame the fire grows bigger and bigger until it's a big blazing ginormous bonfire. That is how you build your dreams, flame by flame until you achieve the big blazing fire.

"All my needs and desires are fulfilled even before I realize
what they are, which will always be for my greatest good and the
most beneficial good of all."

This is your time. What dream is in your heart?

***Discarding Disguises -Beach Glass

This is why we're here. We are all discarding our human disguises of fear, guilt, shame, lack, worry, ego will and mind conditioning and re-connecting with our true inner resonance, of the beloved within. I don't like to use the word: returning. Returning suggests a leaving. We never left. Our true self has faithfully and loyally always been there waiting patiently for our remembering and reunion.

The change and transition happening on earth can feel like the way beach glass is made. What makes glass beach glass? Glass that is tossed around in the ocean enough so it comes out smooth with rounded edges is the best kind of beach glass. If you are a beach glass collector you know if you find a piece of glass on the beach that still has sharp edges you throw it back in the ocean to be tossed around a bit more. I feel like that's how life is in a way. We are the beach glass getting tossed into the big messy pot of soup called life, to be thrown back upon the shore with our jagged edges all smoothed out.

***Tossed Around

If you've ever gotten tossed around in the ocean you know what I'm talking about. While inside the wave you have no idea where up is. It's like you are in a clothes dryer tumbling around. It can be very disorienting and scary. The first time I got tumbled in the waves of Hawaii I was on my way out into the wave break with my HB. He was ahead of me, and we had just gone under a big wave from a large set. He waved me on to hurry up, but I was still tired from the last wave. I looked back at the shore, too far to make it before the next wave, I looked at him, too far to make it! Oh no! I knew I was going to get crushed no matter which direction I went.

So I stood there and waited. I went under the roaring wave dodging the boogie boarders so they wouldn't hit me in the head. The wave tossed me around like a rag doll. My head popped out for a second, I gulped in a big breath of air then got sucked back under to be tossed around some more. Finally I came up, thrown upon the shore. My HB looked so worried, he thought I had gotten hit on the head by the boogie board and drowned. I was in the wave for what seemed like a long while, at least it felt like it.

"I'm ok," I yelled to him, grateful I missed all the lava rocks. That could have been a lot worse, I thought, my heart was racing. I was done for the day. Sometimes that is life. Life can toss you around, kick you in the butt. You need to give yourself a time out, then you get right back in it with more awareness and wisdom. Life is not a spectator sport. Don't wait to be free. Reclaim your personal sovereignty now. It is time.

***Faith-My Soul's in Charge

I have an abundance of faith. I have lived nearly 90% of my life walking in FAITH. That's a lot of 3D uncertainty. Literally in every aspect of my life, what has gotten me through is my faith.

I define Faith as knowing that no matter what happens in the 3D matrix of the illusionary world, God and my higher Self and the universe have my back. I will always be protected, connected and taken care of. I never have to worry about anything. That is my foundation. That is what I truly believe. Do I falter sometimes? Of course, the ego mind comes into play and plants thoughts of doubt and worry into my mind. But I catch it, I catch those thoughts and tell them to go away. Because they are not true and a big fat waste of my time and energy.

If they get really out of control I say to my mind, "Enough! You are not in charge and I'm done with you always wanting to distract me from the present moment. My soul is in charge and that's that."

Sometimes we need to be stern with our ego mind like we are parenting difficult children with firmness, love and respect. And sometimes we just need to surrender and fall into grace.

***Fall back and let the angels catch you in their wings

I was going down the porch stairs backwards, trying to get out of my ohana without my new kitten escaping, forgetting I put a big bag of garbage on the step behind me. When I stepped back I tripped, missed the stair and started falling backwards. Somehow I ended up standing straight up on my feet at the bottom of the stairs. It was like something or someone caught me. My heart was racing. I had to catch my breath. That could have been really really really bad. Oh My Goddess. Thank you, thank you, thank you. Truly, God's got your back.

My HB was my human protector and I loved him for that. I always felt safe with him by my side because I knew he would lay down his life for me. He used to get annoyed with me when I said to him, "Don't worry, I'm fully protected. Archangel Michael is with me." I don't think he really believed, but I did, I do. I don't have fear and I don't walk in fear because I know even if something happens Michael's got my back. No offense against humans, but I have more faith in the divine. I love you Michael!

The Evolution of The Human Spirit

***3D vs 5D: Transmute, Transcend and Ascend

JUST LIKE ARIEL SINGS IN The Little Mermaid… "A whole new world"…This is exactly where we're at- a new world and a new way of being. The potential is unlimited. "The sky's the limit" is another lie. There are no limits.

We are living in two distinct and different realities right now. The timelines are splitting and the bandwidth of each timeline is growing by the day. Those that are waking up are ascending to a higher dimension and those that choose to stay asleep are staying in the lower dimensions. There's no judgment either. It's all about choice – everyone is creating the reality they want.

I've let go of the belief that it's my responsibility to wake anyone up-huge relief. All I can do is share my presence, my light, and my love. I don't talk about myself to anyone unless they ask. Most of my acquaintances and friends here have no idea who I am or what I do. They don't ask and I don't offer. I've learned to stay quiet and conserve my energy, be in my power in a humble and kind way, not boasting or bragging, just being and observing. Observing the old world as it crumbles around and watching the new world unfold. I have enough on my own plate to worry about anyone else's ascension. Those souls that are ready to fly will ascend into the new earth where we will experience once again, heaven on earth. It is not a metaphor. It is real.

I was taking Karma for a walk early one morning at one of our favorite places in the Harbor. This was during my minivan life when life was simple and simpler. It was early so no one else was around. As we walked down the trail I was admiring the special stillness of the early morning energy when I heard the flowers whisper to me, **"Heaven is already here."**

When I refocused my eyes I could see a glow around everything, each tree, each leaf, each flower, each Pili grass. They were glistening with illumination. I got it. I saw through the Maya, and saw the infinity, the divinity and beauty of God everywhere.

***Be Who You Already Are

The Ascension refers to what Source calls a "divine energetic upgrade" that is occurring now on Earth. It is about letting go of old identities and stepping into new identities. The Ascension is about the soul's evolution-becoming who we already are, God in human form.

Ascension means evolving in our consciousness while incarnated on earth. As consciousness evolves, the physical outer world will transform. The higher dimensions that are already here, that are already existing, will become visible. Being in the present moment, tuning in and focusing is how we get there because the truth is that nothing else exists, but the NOW moment. Our perception creates our reality.

A spiritual awakening is often accompanied by a feeling of greater connection to the universe, often through a heightened feeling of love, joy, peace, or oneness with the universe, as well as by increased spiritual sensitivity and spirituality. We can have multiple awakenings in our human body, and each time they can get deeper and more profound. For me the heightened feeling of compassion is how I know I'm ascending into my light Body. I am so in tune to the human experience it's like I can feel everyone's hearts, feel their flame. Sometimes it's overwhelming and I need to be alone in nature to restore my energy because there is so much inner turmoil and suffering in human beings. At times I can feel everyone's pain, it seems.

On the other hand Gaia, Mother Earth, is in the best health she has ever been in. Just as we purify and upgrade our consciousness, our planet does as well. Gaia refreshes herself through weather changes. She is evolving and ascending too. Gaia's heartbeat is measured by the Schumann Resonance which has been steadily increasing over the years. That is because Gaia has already ascended into the fifth dimension and why being in nature is so important. Higher vibrational frequencies cannot lower their vibration as easily as we can raise our vibration. When we spend time in 5D our VF will rise.

There is no more sitting on the fence -it's go time. No more stagnation or even staying at a certain level very long. The process of transformation is moving too rapidly and time is speeding up. Can you feel it? This is part of the Ascension.

Signposts you are moving into 5D:

1. You understand everything is energy vibrating at a different rate. Energy cannot be created or destroyed only change form
2. Feel deep need to connect with nature
3. You feel a ONENESS with everyone and everything in the world
4. You have more vivid or more lucid dreams
5. Your psychic abilities are enhanced
6. You old life is collapsing
7. You feel lost in this world (the 3D world)
8. People are drawn to you more, especially animals and children, which are higher vibration
9. You experience more synchronicities
10. You stop judging yourself and others, be in neutrality

Shifting to 5d can be like a roller coaster. You can experience an array of emotions and experiences, sometimes all within a day. Be extra supportive, understanding, gentle and kind with yourselves. The transition is temporary.

***The Synchronicities are Uncanny.

I met this woman in the ocean at Magic Sands beach. She caught my attention because she was floating on a huge rainbow unicorn raft. I loved her already! I went over to her and introduced myself. We ended up connecting and talking in the ocean for over 30 minutes. She was my age with stage four cancer, but you would have never known with the light that shined through her eyes. She was the brightest light in the ocean. I admired her courage and playfulness. She said she was looking for an energy healer. I replied, "Of course you are, because I am." She took my number but I never heard from her. She lived in another part of the island and didn't get to Kona often.

Months went by and one day I was swimming in the ocean and "B" popped into my mind. I wondered what happened to her, I pondered.

I hope she is ok. I started swimming toward shore and noticed a woman in the ocean smiling and talking to me. I couldn't hear her so I swam closer. She looked at me and said, "I know you." I looked at her and couldn't believe my eyes. It was her!!! I told her she literally just popped into my mind. The healing ocean brought us together again.

This is how life will shift when we are ascending into our holy Self:

Shifting from 3D to 5D:

Pain Body to Light Body
Ego Mind to Heart Center
Thinking to Being
Fragmented to Wholeness
Duality to Unity
Polarity to Oneness
Dark to Light
Bondage to Freedom
Suffering to Joy
Stagnation to Creation
Mental Manifestation to Effortless Flow
Human to Multidimensional New Human
Uncertainty to Clarity
Doubt to Knowing
Lost to the Beloved

Meditation/Reflection suggestion: Visualize the old world, the old you, crumbling away, burning away to ashes. Allow yourself to feel and see the ashes and move the ashes around to alchemize them into new form now. You are the creator of your perceived reality and your heaven on the new earth.

Sitting in a quiet space, ask your soul to download into your being the highest vibration of the Creator (or the totality of you) available to you now. Breathe, because breath is the conductor for the information (light). Then simply allow it to be present with you. Take time even if it's only a few minutes to allow this to be downloaded, embedded and grounded into your being. It is a process of awakening and remembering

The kingdom of heaven is inside of you.

THE PHOENIX HAS RISEN. That is all.

"It's not about rising out of the ashes, like the Phoenix, anymore Beloved. You have been there done that too many times. It's time to just be the fucking fire." ~My Spirit Entourage (even they curse)

***The Annoying Rash

I was reminded once more of having pain as the teacher. I never want to have the skin infection that I had during the writing of this book. It started out with one little annoying itchy spot. It continued on and off for five months. I went to the doctor three times and got three different medications, none of which worked. In addition, I tried every natural remedy I could think of.

Then it ended up over my entire arm. It was scary, painful and swollen. My skin didn't feel like skin anymore. It was hard, oozing with pus and itchy. I thought I might need to amputate my arm. I was so freaked out. The itching kept me up at night, so I dragged during the day. In addition to feeling shame and embarrassment, I felt like a leper and I acted like a hermit because I didn't want to go out in public, but I still had to teach yoga.. I cried out in frustration, I just want this to go away and be normal again! My good sister friend shared that it could be an initiation as a shaman, bringing another level of compassion and empathy toward others, which I totally resonated with.

I thought I could heal it by going to the doctor and getting medication but after three visits my higher self let me know I needed to look this up in my bible. Why did I resist this advice? I knew why, it was too much work! It's easier to go to the doctor and let them tell me what's wrong and fix me then have to take responsibility for my own health. I can be lazy at times too.

The new thought pattern that corrects the imbalance in my body brought so much wisdom. From You Can Heal Your Life, by Louise Hay: **I lovingly protect myself with thoughts of joy and peace.**

Why are they always right!? They know my unstable mind! You can't get a better mantra than that for me right now in my unfolding. The thoughts I was having were inappropriate for my magnificence and was adding to the imbalanced energy of the rash. If I do have thoughts (which obviously I will) they need to be ones that bring joy and peace, and not disharmony, dissatisfaction, discontent, and doubt.

The rest of the new thought pattern or mantra: **The past is forgiven and forgotten. I am free in this moment.**

I was back again on autopilot replaying the past with my mind loops. My body was giving me this very strong communication that I could no longer ignore. I realized that I had been betraying myself, my True God Self that is, for my whole life, even after I had been given direct guidance from Spirit. I spent the day going back over all the guidance, channels, messages and journals I have from the last eight years and listened with new ears. I was in shock how much I missed and how much time it took for their messages to sink in.

I cried for myself. I felt sad. I was finally seeing with new eyes how living my life as a slave to the mind chatter is detrimental and toxic to my soul. I used to cry and feel sorry for myself living unconsciously in a victim mentality. Now I was crying because I was fully awake, seeing for the first time how I had been living veiled in the ego mind selling my God Self short.

"You never left my side," I said to my God Self with tears running down my cheeks, "I'm sorry."

I swore to my God self that I would never do anything again to hurt them/me by not living in the truth of who I am. I am committed to stopping the old patterns of the mind and being in resonance with my heart and my highest joy. And when I focus on something with all my heart I never fail.

I was still feeling bad, thinking I wasted so much time. (Type A personality in full effect) My guides have been giving me the same guidance over and over again in so many different ways. This was the first time I was sad from listening to their advice, so I reached out to my brother.

Sita reminded me: The time is always **NOW.**

I got it right away. I felt much better and immediately let go of feeling bad and refocused on the present moment. That is the higher truth and reality, the only time in NOW. Wasting time is an illusion of the ego mind that keeps us stuck. We think it's too late now to do anything- to follow our dreams, to seek forgiveness, to forgive, to make amends, to call that person, to fix that relationship, to start that project, etc. That is false, false, false, it is never too late. It doesn't matter how old you are in human chronological years, we never die. When we leave the body you think that's it? Over and done? Sorry to tell you but you will bring your unfinished business with you. You got work to do on the other side sista/ braddah.

***The solution to every problem already exists

Back to the skin infection. As much as the new thought pattern resonated with me and helped, I felt it was too late. The pain and swelling had already traveled to my armpit and the infection was at great risk of spreading to the rest of my body. I had to be safe and use common sense. This time the doctor did a culture and prescribed antibiotics. It turned out I had a very bad Staph infection that was turning to the next level. I took antibiotics for seven days and it was 80% gone. I went back to the doctor and asked for another antibiotic which I took for five more days and it went away completely.

I couldn't believe how fast the antibiotics worked! All that needless suffering I put myself through for months! My sister friend said she had the same thing but all over her body for a year! I could not believe it. This is where the statement "Pain is inevitable, but suffering is optional" comes into play. Antibiotics killed it in under two weeks. There was no need for any of my suffering in the end I realized. Why do we do this to ourselves? When the answer and remedy is right there.

Creating this skin infection was twofold. One, was to remind myself of the importance of my thoughts and what I was creating with them, and two, the reminder that sometimes we just need to take the medicine. Healing can be a combination of western medicine and eastern philosophy of shifting our thoughts, it doesn't have to be one or the other.

*** I Am Ease and Grace

When life is uncertain and right now it is so uncertain, and I observe myself falling back into fear based thoughts, I catch myself right from the beginning before they take hold and gather momentum. I say: "Nope, not gonna go there. That was the old me, the old energy, now I am ease and grace and only have thoughts that bring me peace and joy." Period. Next.

The thinking I'm doing is inappropriate, it's disrespectful to my being. This is a new way of looking at my thoughts, I'm taking this stinkin thinkin to a new level now. I need to be more vigilant and serious about my thoughts and conditioned mind loops so I can stay in a high VF and experience the fifth dimension.

I try to catch the thought as soon as I observe it and let it go. Think of climbing a ladder. If you fall from the top it will hurt a lot more than if you fell from the first or second step. It's easier to stop the train of thoughts from the beginning.

Breath deeply. Inhale the light, exhale the thought.
Return to center.

***You are Essential

Essential is a term that has been used a lot during the C story. Being deemed an essential business determined whether your business survived. There's only one thing that's essential in my opinion is being the Beloved of your own heart, knowing God is within and that there is a benevolence, a caring loving Supreme God/Goddess that is always looking out for us. I don't think we really know just how much we are loved. Indeed.

We have more help "on high," then we can possibly imagine. Haumea, which is a dwarf planet in our solar system, is also known as the mother of all goddesses in Hawaii. She is the goddess of goddesses, mother to Pele and many other important Hawaiian deities. Her worship is among the oldest on the Hawaiian islands. Haumea is the mother of fertility and childbirth and symbolizes our individual and collective rebirth. She is working for the psychic unity of humanity across all time and space for the New Earth. She operates at a quantum level, where we are headed as we transcend and ascend into our holy divine Selves. Thank you Haumea for your selfless service to humanity at this time. Mahalo nui loa Haumea.

What is worth seeking and discovering is the truth of the Self.

"Become your own beloved Sacred Hearts. Look within. Cease the looking for external reflection of your holiness.

Dear Lights, becoming the breath of the beloved is the creed that has been divinely bestowed to you by the Creator Itself.

You are your own beloved. When you vibrate this love, you will be the chalice that houses the light for others to sip from and awaken to the beloved within themselves.

It is my highest glory and honor to be walking the way of grace with you".
~Blessed Divine Mother Mary

***For the Greatest Good

I was buying a happy dancing solar sunflower trinket in a Chinese store when the cashier noticed my enormous malachite Buddha ring on my pointer finger. She said, "When it's pointing toward you, it's for you only. When it's turned around, it's for everyone else."

Word. My eyes teared up. It was the profound message my soul needed to hear. I agreed and thanked her for reminding me. I turned it right around, and that is the only way I will wear it now.

Before I knew who I was and why I was here when I was deep in the pain and suffering, what got me up off the floor when all I wanted to do was lie there and die was the simple thought, I might not be able to help myself, but if I can help one other person then my life is worth living.

I didn't know then that I took a vow, made a sacred contract that this lifetime would be dedicated to serving others by going down into the dark pit of suffering and despair to bring back a pearl- a pearl of hope, a pearl of wisdom, a pearl of compassion, a pearl of faith. It makes sense now, I make sense now. You, my friends, are what brought me to my feet from the fetal position on the floor.

***The Gift

After a morning meditation on the beach I gave thanks to Gaia, God, the Aina, all my guardian angels and star family for watching over me. I put my hands on Gaia and sent her my love and gratitude.

It was shell collection day so I said thank you for all the gifts I have received from this beautiful sacred island, when I heard, "You are the gift, dear holy one. You are the gift."

I felt this love energy sweep into my heart and through my body and tears started coming to my eyes. Wow, I feel it. I am the gift. Aren't I? I am the gift.

For the very first time I felt like a gift, that I was truly appreciated from the heavenly realms. It was not just me asking for them to help me, provide me, give me, guide me. It was me being the gift to the universe with all that I do, but more importantly with all that I am.

This came after a yoga class on the beach when I received the ultimate compliment from helping two of my students in a pose, "You have so much kindness, Soulfire. We can feel it." When people can feel my kindness from my presence that makes me very happy and to me is the measure of success.

If you are reading this sunflower and made it to the end I am 100 percent positive that you, dear soul, are a gift too. I might not have met you in person but our souls know each other. And I know that you too give and are kind in so many ways that go unnoticed. (Even though nothing goes unnoticed in the universe.) I want to say thank you for all that you do to make the world a better place. Your light is needed and is appreciated more than you will ever know. As you raise your vibration and frequency the entire planet is uplifted. Thank you.

Take a moment to sit in the energy of my words now. Feel my love and strength and compassion. Breathe it into your heart. I believe in you. You, dear holy one, are the Gift.

Hold the light brave hearts.
This is not the end, for there is no end...

Life is cyclical and we are ONE, you and I, in the now eternal moment that never ends...

To be continued....

A hui a ho, until our hearts meet again,

I love you.

Sparrow Hawk Soulfire

<u>Suggestion for meditation</u>: Tune out the human noise and tune in to the divine noise. The divine noise is all around us. Listen for the wind, the tree branches rustling, the birds singing, the ocean churning, listen for the song. Yes the universe has music. It is playing now, it has never stopped.

I have heard it twice. The first time it woke me up in the middle of the night, about ten years ago when I was doing much spiritual work and exercise every day to get ready for the 2012 shift. I heard the sound of angels singing and harps harping. It sounded like the music that would be played in heaven. It was breathtaking.

Just recently as I was editing this sunflower I heard heaven's music again. It was early morning, still dark outside, I had just woken up and was doing my morning routine when I heard out of my left ear the celestial song of OM with drums and Tibetan bells. At first I thought maybe my neighbor was playing it, but realized I would be the only one on the block listening to this type of music. It was so soothing and beautiful. I was so excited to hear it again with an eastern flair this time.

As you tune your frequency to the God frequency of unity, love, compassion, oneness, joy and peace and use your heart to hear what is being spoken, you will start to hear it. There was once a time when not just the birds sang, but the ocean sang, the earth sang, and we could hear it. Everything that is living has a song, including you. The pumping of your blood, the beating of your heart and the sound of your breath are all being heard as musical notes in outer space.

Your soul is a song,
a Celestial Song of Heaven.

Epilogue

***Trusting Your Own Resonance

If you are not vibrating in your highest resonance you are not being your own Beloved. Just to make sure I was walking my talk, a teaching in my book was reflected back to me during the final phases of the creation of

Soulfire

this sunflower. What I inherently and innately knew to be true made me stop, pause, and question it. Why did I do this? Why would I be questioning my own state of resonance and knowing?

After reflecting on it, I realized it was an old karmic thread that I carried over into this lifetime. In a past life that I shared with you earlier in my sunflower, I altered my teachings and therefore my inherent resonance for fear of how it would be perceived by the external world/audience. This time now I caught myself in the questioning and uncertainty by shining the light of consciousness on the "shadow," the space of not being my own Beloved.

This was not me anymore, I am here to be authentic and to trust myself. When you trust your own Beloved it means you trust your own resonance. Being your own Beloved Is harmonious with being in complete symbiosis with your true state of pure resonance. How do you know if you are vibrating in your highest resonance? For me, when I'm in the ocean I'm in my purest state of resonance; that's when I'm most in touch with my heart and my highest glory and joy. Find yours. Then try to keep that vibration and energy alive during your day in everything you do. Alohaste.

MY HAPPY PLACE

Afterword

"The privilege of a lifetime is to become who you truly are."
~ Carl Gustav Jung

So much has happened since my memoir was published in 2017. When I go back and re-read my writings I realize I am not the same person I was just a couple of years ago. What I was thinking, feeling and being back then, I'm in an entirely new space of consciousness. All of the material I was planning to use for this sunflower I had to write over because it no longer resonated with me. Of course this called for extra work to create sunflower two, but I was happy to see my progress materialize.

We are like the Fibonacci spiral, the mathematical sequence that is found in all living things, in the smallest to the largest objects in nature. Our journey isn't a straight line; it's a spiral. We continuously come back to things we thought we understood and see deeper truths.

Know that change and growth take time. I've been at this since 2001, that's two decades! I've put in the work, sacrifice, dedication and perseverance, and it paid off. The hero's journey is not for the faint of heart. But it's in our DNA and it's our divine birthright to be the best version of ourselves if we so choose.

I traveled across the country from the Atlantic to the Pacific in search of my true love and that is exactly what I found. I found God in my Self, I found my strength, I found my courage, my voice, my power and there's no going back. I received a compliment from a spiritual man here, "It's nice to see a woman standing in her power." He had been observing me at this gathering before I met him. It felt good to hear this because this is exactly what I want to emanate. It's time to bring back the divine feminine energy to the planet by establishing personal peace with the God light that resides within you. You are your own Beloved.

Acknowledgement

"If the only prayer you ever say in your entire life is thank you, it will be enough." ~Meister Eckhart

Without my brother, Dana Livoti, aka Sita, I would not be who I am today. The words 'thank you' seem paltry to everything she has given me. I'm grateful beyond words.

To my daughter, who is my heart and soul...thank you for your unconditional love and support. You are an inspiration.

To Akua for giving me life. I am nothing without you. For all the unconditional love you shower down upon me, I love you.

To Gaia, my sweet mother, you have always been there for me. Each time I cried out in desperation you have healed me and my heart. I love you so much. Thank you for supporting me as I walk upon you each day with so much gratitude in my heart.

To all the angels and my entourage, I feel you, I know you are with me every day guiding me and protecting me. Thank you for being by my side, I could have not done this one without you.

To the sacred Aina here, you have welcomed me with open arms and have supported my journey. I love you so much and every day I will give back in the spirit of aloha as much as you have given me.

To my new friend and sister, Becky, you are rad. Thank you for helping me edit my sunflower with your insight and intelligence.

To Shawna, thank you for adding your creativity and helping me create the stunning photos for my book, as well as capturing the unicorns!

To Wendy Jarva, my amazing friend, who has always been there for me. You embody true friendship and loyalty. I treasure you with all my heart. Thank you for helping me create the badass covers for my books.

To LP, my dear sister friend and fairy webmaster. Thank you for all you do to help me in my divine mission.

Thank you so much, Jason and Vidya EbookPbook.com for your help in presenting this sacred work of art from my heart to the world.

To Lisa Mintz, my dear friend, the artist and creative engine behind my logos. Thank you for supporting me and helping me bring the light and message of the sunflower and lighthouse to the world.

To my soulmate, Hawaiian Beloved, thank you for coming into my life and helping me become the beloved of my own heart. Without you I would still have been lost. I love you eternally and forever. You will always be a part of my heart. And thank you for your amazing photography and advice.

There is no end to the gratitude I hold in my heart. Every day with every breath I will continue to give thanks and praise.

Aloha Ke Akua God is love and so are you.

About the Author

Galactic Cosmic Goddess Warrior Light and Spiritual Human Being devoted to serving humanity by pioneering the New Light of the New Earth and awakening the divine within each soul through sharing her transformational life experiences and new spiritual technology. For more info please visit her on the world wide web: www.igniteyoursoulfire.com

Books By This Author

Fearless Freedom Becoming SoulFire

This is the story about a girl who changed her life. She has embraced her spiritual name, SoulFire, on every level, and has courageously written this autobiography in hopes that it will inspire, heal, and awaken others to the Divinity within their free hearts. She understands what it's like to walk the Earth feeling alone, lost, unloved, and unwanted, and has risen above the anguishes of abandonment throughout every chapter of her life. She also knows that we did not come here to suffer, we came here to thrive. As spiritual alchemists, we need the darkness to find the light and our true freedom. Being a spiritual seeker since childhood, she has never stopped questioning, studying, and learning. Referencing the ancient teachings of yoga and timeless wisdom, with vulnerability and quirky humor, she shares her experiences of being a single mother, growing up as an adopted child, healing her back and neck disabilities, going through bankruptcy, and at times feeling utter despair. However, she has risen above it all, like the Phoenix Bird, and is a walking demonstration of how one can overcome adversities by using them as portals for discovery. We all have the power to heal ourselves. As we heal, the world heals. The dawning of the new Earth is here now, beckoning us to awaken from our spiritual slumber, and re-remember our Divine magnificence! Journey into your authentic Self through these pages. Rediscover the beautiful, powerful, and loving soul that you truly are. You are the cage and you are the key. Ignite your soul fire and be free!

The SoulFire Awakening

Join the author, Soulfire, as she takes you through a journey to ignite your soul's fire with this empowering, revolutionary and dynamic moving meditation. Birthed from the space of shadow into the reemergence of light, SoulFire Awakening represents the movement to the words of her inspirational memoir: *Fearless Freedom Becoming SoulFire.* It is a simple yet sacred, powerful and purposeful sequence using special breathing techniques and easy poses that will help you realign, reenergize, refocus, rebalance and reactivate your health and vibration to your divine light body. User friendly for all ages. Awaken to your divine magnificence and be rooted and free.

Made in the USA
Middletown, DE
01 June 2023

31512840R00139